WATERLOO LOCAL SCHOOL
PRIMARY LIBRARY

W9-ACR-847

WATERLOO LOCAL SCHOOL
PRIMARY LIBRARY

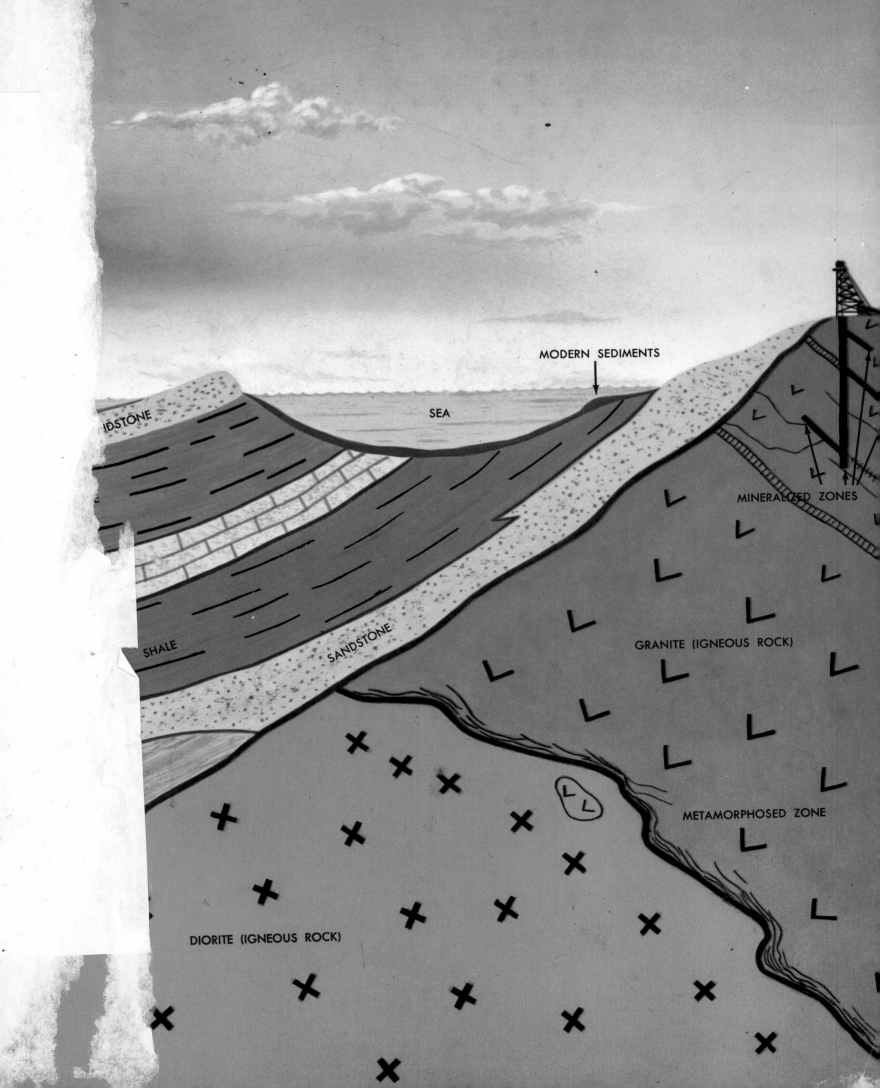

MODERN SEDIMENTS

SEA

IDSTONE

SHALE

SANDSTONE

MINERALIZED ZONES

GRANITE (IGNEOUS ROCK)

METAMORPHOSED ZONE

DIORITE (IGNEOUS ROCK)

THE PLANET
WE LIVE ON

Written by FELIX SUTTON

Illustrated by JOHN HULL

With an Introduction by SHELDON JUDSON,
Associate Professor in Geology, Princeton University

GROSSET & DUNLAP · Publishers · NEW YORK

525

WATERLOO LOCAL SCHOOL
PRIMARY LIBRARY

Introduction

This is the story of a planet. It isn't the only planet in the skies, nor is it even the biggest. We know of eight others that revolve around our star, the sun — and four, perhaps five, of these are larger. Astronomers tell us that there are probably millions of more planets wheeling around other stars. But this book tells about the planet we know best — our planet — the planet we call "Earth."

The earth is but a speck in the vastness of space and we already know more about it than we will probably ever know about any other planet. Its story is a long one — between four and five billion years, we believe. In these pages you will find out something about this history. You will learn about volcanoes and mountains, glaciers and deserts, the ocean depths and the earth's rich store of mineral wealth. You will read about some of the living things that have fashioned their homes beneath the earth's surface, about the caves in which prehistoric men once lived and about man-made "caves" in use today.

Although we know a great deal about the earth, there are still more unanswered questions than answered ones. You will find some of these yet-to-be-answered puzzles in this book. Some of them will be solved in your lifetime and some of you may even help to provide the answers.

Sheldon Judson
Associate Professor in Geology
Princeton University
Princeton, N. J.

© 1960, by Grosset & Dunlap, Inc.
All rights reserved under International and Pan-American Copyright Conventions.
Published simultaneously in Canada.   Printed in the United States of America.

Contents

The earth was created from clouds of cosmic dust.

How the Earth Was Born

EVER since man has been intelligent enough to be curious, he has wondered about the planet he lived on. What was it made of? How was it made? How long ago was it born?

The answer lay in the opening sentences of the Old Testament: "In the beginning God created the heaven and the earth. And the earth was without form, and void. . . ."

But it was not until astronomers like Copernicus and Galileo and Kepler discovered how the planets move around the sun — and Sir Isaac Newton showed how each particle of matter in the universe exerts a gravitational pull on every other particle — that scientists could begin to unlock the secret contained in these two simple sentences.

After the invention of the telescope, about 1609, astronomers were able to observe the behavior of the planets closely for the first time. And in doing so, they began to make some remarkable discoveries.

They found that all the planets in the solar system move in the same direction around the sun — that each planet spins on its axis in the same direction as its orbit around the sun — that the sun, too, rotates in the same direction as that in which its planets move around it — and that the planets themselves are spaced at fairly regular intervals from each other.

Thus, scientists started to reason, if all the planets behave so much alike, they all must have been formed at about the same time and in the same way. If this were not the case, there would be no logical reason for them to have an identical behavior pattern.

In 1749, a French scientist, Buffon, advanced the theory that at one time a wayward star had had a near collision with our sun. The gravitational force of this star pulled out huge masses of the sun's gas, which later solidified and became the planets.

Nearly half a century later, in 1796, another Frenchman, La Place, offered a quite different theory which, even at that early date, came very close to what we now believe to be the truth. He theorized that the sun had once exploded and flung off a vast cloud of gas and cosmic dust. As this nebula of fiery gases began to condense, it spun faster and faster around the sun until great rings of it were thrown off by centrifugal force. In time these rings contracted and became solid, and eventually evolved into the individual planets.

Astronomers have yet to agree among themselves about the details of the earth's creation, but most modern scientists believe that the sun, along with all its planets and their individual moons, were formed at the same time. They think that, more than a hundred billion years ago, what is now our solar system was a cloud of cold dust particles. Then, in response to the law of gravity, these particles came together to form a huge, whirling disk. As it spun, the disk separated into rings. The nucleus of the disk became the sun, and the particles in the outer

rings collected themselves together into dense concentrations. As these masses grew in size, they attracted smaller masses, and at last became great fiery balls of gas and molten liquid. Then they began to cool and condense and take on a solid form, and at last, after many eons of time, became the planets.

This theory explains, among other mysteries, why the sun and all the planets rotate and orbit in the same direction, and also why the positions of the planets in the solar system are so evenly spaced.

And so, about four or five billion years ago, our planet earth — which in the beginning was "without form, and void," nothing but a cloud of cosmic dust swirling through the heavens — was born.

How the Earth's Age
Is Determined

IT WAS not until very recent times that scientists had any reliable yardstick by which to measure the age of the earth.

More than a hundred years ago, pioneers in the science of geology began to examine the rock formations

of the earth's surface. They found that these surface rocks were often laid layer upon layer, and that each layer contained different kinds of fossil remains of animal and vegetable life.

They discovered, for example, fossil remains of sea animals in the firm rock of some of our highest mountains. They also found evidences of once subtropical climates in what are now polar regions. They concluded, therefore, that the earth's surface had seen many changes. We know that the surface of our planet is changing today, but very slowly: rivers dry up or grow wider; points of land are washed away; rocks slide down from mountain tops and reduce the mountain's size; volcanoes create new mountains.

And so these early geologists reasoned that the earth's features had changed just as slowly in the past. They concluded that it must have taken many millions of years to change a sea bottom into a mountain or a subtropical jungle into an arctic waste.

But it was not until the beginning of the twentieth century that scientists discovered a tool that could tell them almost exactly how old the earth really is. This tool is called *radioactivity,* and when it was found, the age of the earth began to be computed not in millions, but in billions, of years.

Explained simply, radioactivity means that certain elements, such as uranium, decay over the years and break down into simpler elements, such as lead. This rate of decay can be measured in terms of years.

Some rocks tested by this radioactivity method have proved to be about three billion years old. We know that older rocks must exist, and so scientists now generally believe that the earth must be somewhere between four and five billion years of age.

This estimate of the earth's age has been checked by the radioactive reading of meteors that have landed on our planet from outer space, since, as we have said, scientists believe that the meteors were formed at the same time as the earth.

These meteor fragments, too, give a radioactive reading of between four and five billion years.

And so this figure — give or take a billion years — is generally accepted as the approximate age of the planet we live on.

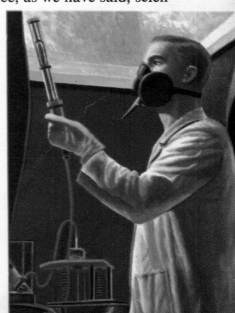

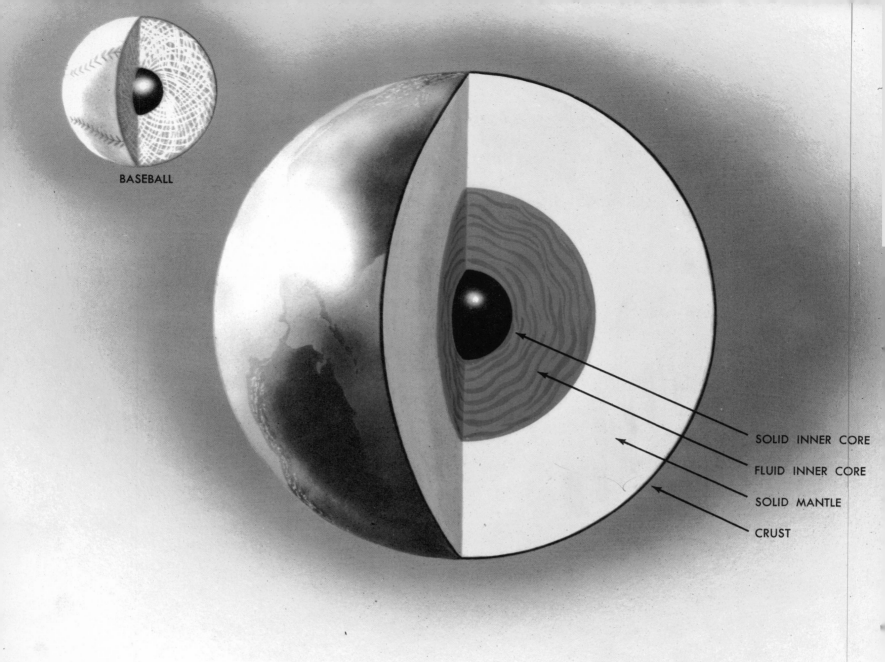

BASEBALL

SOLID INNER CORE

FLUID INNER CORE

SOLID MANTLE

CRUST

The Interior of the Earth

AS THE molten mass of the infant earth cooled and began to solidify, the heaviest elements sank into the center of the globe. The lightest elements were pushed upward toward the surface, and those intermediate in weight found their proper places in between.

As the ages passed, the crust of the earth — the surface on which we walk — cooled and became firm and hard. But it was obvious even in ancient times that the earth's interior was quite different from its surface. Volcanoes spewed out smoke and flame and molten rock from somewhere deep inside the earth, and geysers shot up streams of boiling water and poisonous gases.

It was a great many centuries before man was able to solve this riddle of what lay under the earth's hard, cold surface.

We now know that the earth is constructed something like a baseball.

If you were to cut a baseball in two, you would see that it has a core of solid rubber. Wrapped around this inner core are a great many layers of heavy string. This string binding is solid, yet it is not as solid as the rubber core, for it will move and give and sometimes alter its shape under pressure. The outer covering is a thin layer of horsehide, which holds in all the rest of the ball.

Now a cross section of the earth, as it is pictured on this page, is a little more complicated than that of a baseball. But you can see that basically it is much the same.

The solid-rock covering of the earth, called the *crust* — which in turn is covered in most places by an extremely thin layer of soil — is only between ten and thirty miles thick.

Under this thin crust is a very thick layer of a different kind of rock, which is known as the earth's *mantle*. The rock of the mantle is solid, but it is solid in the same way that the string wrapping of a baseball is solid. Under pressure it will move slightly and change position. The mantle extends to a depth of 1,800 miles.

Enclosed by the mantle is the earth's *core*. Unlike the center of a baseball, the earth's center is made up of two parts: an outer core and an inner core.

Both are composed of metal — predominantly iron, with some nickel. But the outer core is liquid, and the inner core is solid.

The total distance from the earth's surface to the center of its inner core averages 3,960 miles.

As the depth of the earth increases, the temperature goes up, but not in proportion to the depth.

At the upper edge of the mantle, the earth's body heat rises from our pleasant, livable temperatures at the surface to about 2,000 degrees Fahrenheit, approximately the melting point of certain kinds of rocks. It is from this level that molten rock, called *magma,* collects in pockets and spews up through cracks in the crust to erupt from volcanoes in the form of lava.

At the very center of the core, the temperature is probably 8,000 degrees, not much less than the temperature on the surface of the sun.

You may wonder why the inner core, although solid, should be hotter than the outer core, which consists of the same metals but is liquid.

The answer lies in the fact that the pressure at the center of the inner core is more than 45,000,000 pounds per square inch, literally squeezing the core into a solid mass. And the "liquid" core surrounding it, although possessing the qualities of a fluid, is unlike any liquid we have ever seen, and is probably far denser than our surface rocks.

How We "See" the Earth's Interior

THE deepest hole ever bored into the earth was an oil well that went down about four miles. This is only about one seventh of the way through the earth's crust and only one thousandth of the way to the earth's center. How then can our scientists "see" what our planet's interior is like?

The answer is — earthquakes!

To the people they directly affect, earthquakes are terrible and deadly things. But to scientists, they provide the best key for unlocking the secrets of the inside of the earth.

Every time an earthquake occurs — and there are about 150,000 each year throughout the world — it sends out shock waves all through the earth, even to the deepest parts. When these waves come to the surface again, they are picked up and recorded by extremely sensitive instruments, called seismographs, which are located in laboratories at hundreds of places around the globe.

Basically earthquake waves are of two kinds: P (primary) waves and S (secondary) waves.

P waves travel faster than S waves. P waves go through liquids, but S waves can't. The speeds of both P waves and S waves vary according to the depth of the earth they have penetrated. And both behave differently as they pass through rocks of differing composition.

Thus, by studying the behavior of the P and S waves, the depths at which they have been reflected and bent, the distance they have traveled from their point of origin, and the time it has taken them to make the journey, scientists are able to chart the insides of the earth — in much the same way that a doctor uses X-rays to see what the inside of the human body looks like.

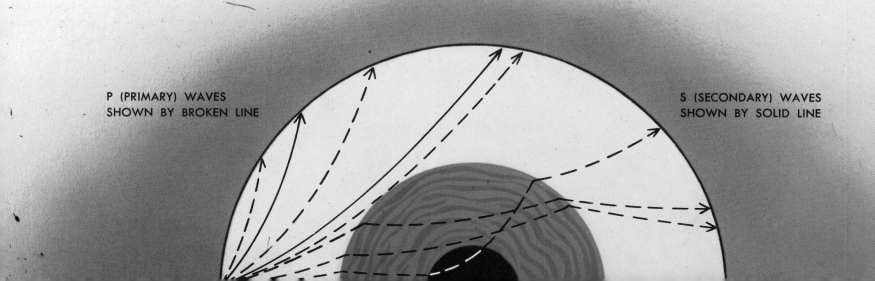

P (PRIMARY) WAVES
SHOWN BY BROKEN LINE

S (SECONDARY) WAVES
SHOWN BY SOLID LINE

Ancient Egyptians believed a flat earth was covered by a metal canopy of sky through which the gods suspended the shining moon and stars.

Hindu priests taught that the earth was a flat disc, supported by four elephants standing on the back of a gigantic turtle.

Ancient Beliefs About the Earth

WHEN WE stand on a hill and look out over the surface of the earth, the planet we live on *seems* to be a very different thing from what it actually is.

To our eyes it appears to be a reasonably flat expanse of land, dotted by hills and dimpled by valleys, extending from one horizon to the other. The sun moves across it by day, and the moon and stars circle it at night. We seem to be the center of everything, and everything moves around us.

Even in this modern day it is difficult for us to accept a fact that our eyes tell us isn't so. It is sometimes difficult for us to understand that the earth is not a flat surface at all, but instead is a large round ball with a center as hot as the surface of the sun — that the ground on which we stand, which seems so serene and quiet and still on a hot summer afternoon, is actually spinning around at the furious rate of a thousand miles an hour — that our earth is racing around the sun at better than 66,000 miles an hour — and that, along with the sun and all the planets, it is whizzing around the outside edge of the Milky Way at nearly half a million miles an hour, a speed almost impossible to imagine.

It is no wonder, then, that ancient man formed many weird, and to us ridiculous, ideas of what the earth was like. But we must remember that most of the ancient peoples were in almost total ignorance of natural laws.

When the earliest civilizations began to develop and mysticism and superstition became the dominant forces in human life, the priests and wise men tried to explain the earth and the sun and the stars in terms of their own limited existence and their supernatural beliefs.

The ancient Egyptians, for example, lived in the narrow valley of the Nile River. They were surrounded by impenetrable deserts and stark forbidding mountains, and there was no way for them to know that any other human beings existed, nor that there was any other part of the world except their own confined valley. Therefore, they pictured themselves as being the center of the universe.

They believed that the earth was a flat, level floor, with Mother Nile running through it to give it life. The earth was walled in on all sides by mountain peaks. The Egyptians had a knowledge of metal, and since the clear, blue, cloudless sky above the desert had a metallic sheen, they thought it was a vast metal ceiling spread over the earth and resting its four corners on four mountain tops.

At night the gods lowered brightly lit lamps through holes in the metal ceiling — these were the stars and the moon — so that the Egyptians might have some small amount of light after the sun god had passed by.

The Chinese pictured the earth as being carried along on the back of a huge toad. Whenever the toad moved, it caused a great earthquake.

Eratosthenes of Greece measured the circumference of the earth about 300 B.C. — and missed the correct figure by only a few hundred miles!

Since the elephant was a sacred symbol to the ancient Hindus, they conceived of the earth as a flattened disk supported by four elephants. These elephants stood on the back of a giant turtle. And the turtle in turn rested on the coils of a mighty serpent that was floating on the surface of a mystic sea.

In ancient China the priests taught that the earth was carried on the back of a monstrous toad, and that whenever the toad moved, it caused an earthquake.

The people of ancient Greece, on the other hand, were advanced a great many centuries beyond their times in art, philosophy, literature, and science. They were a seafaring merchant people, and so they knew something of the world as it existed beyond the boundaries of their own islands.

As early as 580 B.C. their scientists had deduced that the earth was not a flat island floating in some mysterious sea or supported on the back of a celestial animal. Instead, they knew that it was a sphere suspended in the sky. However, they believed that it was the center of the universe, with the sun and all the stars revolving around it.

Aristotle observed that as a ship moved away from shore, it seemed to sink over the rim of the earth. First, you could see the whole ship. Then, as it got farther away, the hull disappeared and you could see only the sails. At last, these too disappeared over the horizon. He also noticed that the earth cast a circular shadow on the moon.

Aristarchus of Samos, who lived in the third century B.C., reasoned that the sun was the center of the universe and that the earth and all the planets revolved around it.

Thus, he became the first man to learn the true nature of our solar system. He even made an attempt to calculate, by means of trigonometry, the distances from the earth to the sun and the moon. His theory was sound, but because he had no reliable instruments, his figures were far from correct.

One of the most amazing of the ancient Greek scientists was Eratosthenes, who lived at about the same time as Aristarchus. He actually calculated the circumference of the earth and came surprisingly close to what it was later discovered to be! He observed the angle of the sun at high noon on a certain day at Alexandria, Egypt. He then measured the sun's angle at the same time, on the same day of the year, at what is now the site of the Aswan Dam, some 500 miles south. Using geometric equations, he determined that the earth's circumference was 28,800 miles. Today we know that the correct figure is 24,847 miles.

Greek culture, however, was lost in the upheavals of war and conquest, and the knowledge of the universe which these great men were slowly beginning to bring to light was hidden from the world by nearly two thousand years of intellectual darkness.

In 1492, when Columbus proposed to find a shorter route to the East Indies by sailing west, most Europeans still believed that the earth was a flat and isolated island, floating on a terrible and mysterious sea which was guarded by fearful monsters and over whose edge a ship would fall into some eerie and unknown limbo if it ventured too far from shore.

The Earth Is a Magnet

THE FACT that the earth is a gigantic magnet was discovered by the Chinese more than 1,500 years ago, but they didn't know what they had discovered. They knew only that if a needle was stroked by a lodestone and then mounted on a pivot, it would always point north and south.

As far back as 1180, an Englishman named Alexander Neckam wrote an essay in which he described how a magnetized needle could enable sailors to steer a true course when the sky was overcast and they could not see the stars. Neckam supposed, however, that the needle was attracted by the North Star.

This belief persisted until the year 1600 when Sir William Gilbert, an English doctor, theorized that the earth itself is a magnet and that the magnetic needle was attracted to the North Pole. He also believed that the magnetic North Pole was not the same as the geographic North Pole.

We know today that the magnetic pole is about a thousand miles from the true, or geographic, pole.

There are a great many things about the earth's magnetism that scientists still do not know. But one widely held theory is that the magnetic field is set up by electrical currents deep within the earth's liquid core. Many believe that these currents are probably created when minerals of differing electrical properties and different temperatures come together. It would seem most reasonable that this would take place at a point where the silicate rock of the earth's mantle meets the molten metal of the core.

If this is true, it means that there is a huge, natural electric generator in the center of the earth which is constantly turning mechanical energy (the earth's rotation and the movement of the liquid core) into electrical energy. This theory is strengthened by the facts that all magnetic fields are the result of electrical currents and all electrical currents are surrounded by magnetic fields.

The aurora borealis — or northern lights

525

WATERLOO LOCAL SCHOOL
PRIMARY LIBRARY

If you lay a piece of paper over a toy bar magnet and then sprinkle iron filings on top of the paper, you will see that the filings form a pattern of little arcs around each end, or pole. This pattern follows the lines of force that the magnet exerts.

In the same way, the magnetism of the earth sets up lines of force around the globe.

One dramatic example of these lines of magnetic force can sometimes be seen on clear, cold winter nights when the northern lights glow on the horizon underneath the North Star.

The northern lights are caused by the fact that electrified particles are constantly showering down toward the earth from the sun. The earth's magnetic field, which extends far out into space, captures these particles and spins them around the lines of magnetic force. Since they come closest to earth at the poles, they set up an eerie glow as they enter the earth's atmosphere.

Polar icecap 600 million years ago   Polar icecap 200-300 million years ago   Present location of polar icecap

The Shifting Poles

FROM THEIR studies of ancient rocks in South America, South Africa, India, and Australia, geologists have long known that these lands, which now have a nearly tropical climate, lay buried beneath vast sheets of glacier ice some 230,000,000 years ago. They know, too, from the discovery of fossil plants and animals, that the present lands of the Arctic and Antarctic once enjoyed a much warmer climate.

These facts suggested to scientists over forty years ago that the poles had shifted their positions since the earth's beginning. Very recently new evidence from a different source seems to confirm this theory.

Scientists can now measure the very weak magnetism of many different types of rock. Some of this weak magnetism is left over from the magnetism originally in the rocks when they were first formed many millions of years ago. Since this "fossil" magnetism does not point to our modern magnetic poles, we can only assume that the magnetic poles have shifted since the rocks were formed. And since we know that the magnetic poles can never be more than about a thousand miles from the true, or geographic, poles, then it follows that the geographic poles have also shifted.

The drawing above shows how the North Pole has shifted from place to place on the face of the planet we live on. Half a billion years ago the pole was near the equator in the eastern Pacific. And 170 million years ago, early in the Age of Dinosaurs, it lay in an area of Siberia.

So, since the poles have shifted in the past, there is no reason to believe that they will not continue to do so in the future — and that, hundreds of millions of years from now, the polar icecap may be somewhere in Connecticut or Kansas, while Alaska has a tropical climate.

15

The earth quakes when the rock beneath the surface suddenly cracks and moves. This cutaway picture of a margin of a continent shows earthquake waves radiating outward from a zone of movement along a break — a "fault" — in the earth's crust.

Earthquakes — Why They Happen

MOST OF the time the surface of the planet we live on is firm and steady and secure. But sometimes the earth shakes and trembles, jarring masses of rock loose from the mountainsides, opening up shallow fissures in the ground, and knocking down buildings in towns and cities.

As we have seen, the thin outer crust of the earth is formed of uneven layers of different kinds of rock. This rock is subject to constant pressures, not only from the layers of rock that lie above them, but more importantly from forces within the earth which even today geologists cannot fully explain. These pressures tend to distort the rock and cause it to change shape.

The pressures from within the earth persist over long periods of time. But eventually, if they are great enough, some of the rock may suddenly break — in the same way

that a stick will give for a while when you bend it with your hands, and then suddenly snap in two. The rock breaks apart and snaps back just as the two broken ends of the stick do. This sudden snap jars the earth's crust and causes it to shake. We call this an earthquake.

The place where the rock breaks and moves is called a *fault*.

Earthquakes can occur anywhere around the globe. But they are most common around the edges of the Pacific Ocean — up the western coast of South and North America, and then back down the western rim of the Pacific through Japan, the Philippines and the South Sea Islands.

Another *earthquake zone* lies along the Mediterranean Sea and extends into the Near East, but it is much less active than the Pacific Ocean area.

Tidal Waves

SOMETIMES, when an earthquake takes place on the bottom of the sea, it causes a tidal wave.

At first, the change in the level of the sea bottom sucks the water away from the shoreline, often clear out of sight. This is the danger signal. For the sea will soon return in a gigantic wave which grows higher as it moves

in toward shallow water, occasionally reaching a height of 100 feet and a speed of over 300 miles an hour!

Obviously nothing can stand in the way of such a tremendously powerful wall of onrushing water, and tidal waves have caused a great deal of death and destruction, especially in the Pacific.

Crest of a tidal wave

How Mountains Are Formed

WHEN WE look up at the snow-covered peak of a mountain that thrusts its rocky head high into the sky, it seems to be the most permanent and lasting thing in all the world. Poets have written about the "everlasting hills" and the "eternal mountains."

But, like every other part of the earth's surface, mountains are slowly but surely changing. Old mountains are being worn down and washed away by the erosion of wind and rain. And new mountain ranges are rising up.

Let us see how new mountains are formed.

We can easily picture a volcano building its cone higher and higher until it creates a towering peak. Some famous volcanic mountains are Kilimanjaro in Africa, Vesuvius in Italy, Fujiyama in Japan, and the many peaks that mark our fiftieth state, Hawaii.

The newest volcanic mountain of any size is Paricutin in Mexico. Only a few years ago, in 1943, the site on which Paricutin now stands was a level cornfield. Then one day smoke and flames and lava came spurting up out of the ground, and the black lava ash began building up into a mountain. Today the peak of Paricutin towers more than 1,000 feet above the former cornfield.

While volcanic cones form mountains, these peaks only reflect the unrest that is constantly going on deep beneath the earth's surface. These sub-surface disturbances, which include earthquakes and the upward pushing of molten rock to form volcanoes, are similar to the forces that have built the world's great mountain chains.

The picture becomes clearer if we think of volcanoes as blisters on the back of a newly forming or young mountainous area.

If we were able to slice open a mountain range such as the Rockies or the Andes or the Alps, we would see that the layers of rock had been broken and crumbled. We would find also that many of the rocks that now tower thousands of feet above sea level were originally formed at the bottom of the ocean. We know this because the fossil remains of sea animals have been found in rocks on the topmost peaks.

From these facts, then, we would have to conclude that the mountains were formed from the rocks of ancient sea floors and that powerful forces within the earth broke and folded and raised these rocks into their present position.

As soon as the mountains rose above the sea, *erosion* began to destroy them. Swift-flowing streams and slow-moving glaciers began tearing away at the mountains. Landslides moved rocks and earth from higher to lower places.

Geologists believe that the surface of the earth is continually changing in this way — that the earth's crust is in constant motion, like the waves on the surface of the sea. But instead of rising up and leveling off again in a split second, as sea waves do, the movement of the "waves" of the earth's surface — the mountains and the valleys — takes hundreds of millions of years.

The San Francisco Earthquake

THE COAST of California is subject to more earthquake shocks than any other part of the continental United States. Two or three times in an average year, light tremors, usually lasting only a few seconds, rattle windowpanes and knock dishes from kitchen shelves.

On several occasions during the past century, the city of San Francisco has been struck by shocks violent enough to crack walls and topple buildings. This is partly because the city lies on top of the San Andreas Fault, a zone of faulting and cracking in the earth's crust that extends for several hundred miles along the Pacific Coast.

By far the worst of these California earthquakes came early in the morning of April 18, 1906. The first violent shock, which came without warning, caused buildings all over the city to collapse. It was followed five minutes later by another trembling of the ground which ripped up pavements and streetcar tracks, and left the city an almost total ruin.

Even worse than the earthquake damage was the destructive effect of a fire that swept over the city in the wake of the earthquake. The quake had broken all the water mains, leaving firemen with no means of fighting the blaze. The fire raged for four days, and when it finally burned itself out, hardly a structure in the city was standing, and more than 300,000 people were left homeless. The amount of energy released by the San Francisco earthquake was equal to that of a million atom bombs.

Recent surveys have indicated that the San Andreas Fault is still bending and storing up energy that may be released in future earthquakes.

San Francisco in ruins — April 18, 1906

The Tokyo Earthquake

ONE OF the greatest earthquake disasters of all time took place in Tokyo, the capital of Japan, on September 1, 1923.

The ground under the city shook and trembled violently for several minutes — "like a small boat in windy weather," as one survivor described it — and as a result knocked down most of the city's homes and buildings. As in the case of San Francisco, the quake was followed by a fire that completed the nearly total destruction.

Almost a quarter of a million people were killed, injured, or reported missing after the quake and fire, and more than half a million buildings were destroyed.

At one point, about 40,000 frightened people were huddled together on a river bank in an effort to escape the flames that were closing in all around them. They were packed so tightly in the narrow space that it was impossible for anyone to move. Suddenly a whirlwind created by the superheated air swept over them. Seconds later, only 2,000 of the 40,000 refugees were left alive. The rest had been burned to death by the intense heat or suffocated by the smoke and fumes.

After the earthquake, Tokyo was rebuilt, with many modern, quake-proof buildings in place of the former flimsy structures of wood and stone.

An Earthquake That Made a Desert Bloom

MOST EARTHQUAKES bring nothing but destruction and misery to the people they affect. But to the Cocopah Indians of the Santa Caterina Desert in Lower California, the violent quake of February 9, 1956, was a blessing in disguise.

The quake cracked walls and shattered windowpanes in Los Angeles and San Diego, but the most severe shocks were felt in the desert south of the Mexican border.

The earthquake, which ran parallel to the lower portion of the San Andreas Fault, cracked the earth in all directions. It changed the outlines of existing cliffs, thrust up new ones out of the ground, and left deep fissures in the surface for miles around.

The Santa Caterina Desert had been a barren, water-less wilderness, and life for the Indians was hard as they tried to scrape a living out of the hostile soil. But in the midst of all the damage to the land, one of the cracks in the earth tapped an underground reservoir, and a well of fresh, sweet water spurted out of the ground.

The Indians dug irrigation ditches across the desert from this unexpected water supply and began to prepare the area for farming.

Today, thanks to the freak earthquake which for once did more good than harm, that part of the desert is fertile farmland and the Indians are more prosperous than they have ever been.

The Great Rift of Africa

THE BIGGEST, longest crack in the earth's surface is the Great Rift Valley of Africa. It begins at the shores of the Red Sea in French Somaliland and winds like a monstrous serpent through Ethiopia, Kenya, and Tanganyika, finally ending in Mozambique.

Millions of years ago, a tremendous upheaval of the crust ripped the rock apart to create an enormous fissure which in places is more than fifty miles wide, with sheer stone walls a mile high on either side.

Most of Africa's great central lakes lie inside the Great Rift — Lake Tanganyika, Lake Albert, Lake Edward, and Lake Kiva. Parts of the valley floor are lush grasslands, which provide shelter for huge herds of wild animals, as well as pasture for the cattle and goats of the native tribesmen. Other parts are barren and rocky, with dry lake beds which now have deposits of soda and salt.

A large number of extinct volcanoes exist within the Great Rift, as well as several smaller ones which are still active from time to time. Scientists say, however, that the formation of the Great Rift was due, not to volcanic activity, but to rock-faulting on a stupendous scale.

Actually, the crack that is the Great Rift extends beneath the Red Sea as an undersea canyon and on into Jordan and Syria in Asia. The Dead Sea in Palestine — whose surface lies 1,300 feet below sea level and whose water is 26 per cent salt — lies inside the Great Rift.

Altogether, the Great Rift is about 4,000 miles long.

The Grand Canyon

THE MOST famous gash in the surface of the earth is the Grand Canyon of the Colorado River, in Arizona. Unlike the Great Rift, it was not a fault in the crust — its rock did not rip apart. Instead, it was slowly worn away, or eroded, by the river.

A few millions of years ago the Colorado Plateau area was not far above sea level. Then, very slowly, the region rose upward as a flat tableland. Unlike the Rocky Mountains to the northeast, the crust did not buckle and fold as it rose, forming a jagged mountain range. Instead, its elevation was so gradual and peaceful that the layers of rock were hardly bent, and they are still almost horizontal, even though the top of the plateau is now nearly a mile and a half above sea level.

When the plateau was first lifted upward, a system of winding rivers ran across it. Among these was the ancestral Colorado. The land rose up in such a leisurely manner that the course of the river was not changed, but dug itself deeper into its original path.

The river, which now flows through the bottom of a magnificent gorge which is a mile deep, 217 miles long, and as much as 18 miles wide, did not start at the top and wear its way down. In fact, geologists believe that the stream was never much higher than it is now. Instead, as the land rose, the river cutting through it maintained just about its original level.

To make this point clearer, some geologists have likened the Colorado Plateau to a gigantic layer cake, and the river to a knife cutting through it. But instead of the knife cutting downward through the cake, the cake has pushed itself upward against the cutting edge of the knife, while the knife itself has remained almost stationary.

Today, if you were to ride on a mule along the narrow twisting trails that lead from the rim to the canyon floor, you would pass a living history of the development of life on earth. Through fossil remains embedded in the various layers of sedimentary rock, it is possible to follow the story of the evolution of plant and animal life for hundreds of millions of years.

First, you would see the primitive algae, the world's very first form of life, which developed in the sea when the whole plateau was covered by water. Then higher up on the walls you would find the fossilized remains of primitive sea animals. After them come the amphibians, the first animals that emerged from the sea and took up life on land. You can see their tracks and the imprints of their bodies, originally made in mud that has now turned to stone. At last, higher up on the rim, are the fossil tracks of the first reptiles and dinosaurlike creatures — as well as early ferns and primitive pine trees.

The Colorado River is still at its work of cutting through the plateau, and it is probable that the plateau itself is still gently rising. Geologists believe that in some far-off future time the entire plateau will be eroded into a range of rugged mountains.

More than a scenic wonder, Grand Canyon has recorded a fabulous diary of earth's life forms and geological changes.

Mount Okmok, Aleutian Islands

Volcanoes

WE HAVE seen that the solid rock layers that form the earth's crust are thicker in some places than in others, and that directly underneath them the earth's temperature is hot enough to melt rock. This molten rock is known as *magma*.

At certain places under the crust, magma collects in reservoirs or pools. As this magma wells up out of the interior of the earth, it pushes various gases ahead of it. And as these gases become more and more tightly compressed, they exert a tremendous pressure against the underside of the crust.

If this occurs at a place where the crust is weak, or where an ancient earthquake has created a fault or break in the rock, the mixture of gas and magma breaks through the crack and erupts on the earth's surface in the form of lava — in much the same way that a carbonated drink will blow a loose cork out of a bottle if it is heated or shaken up.

As the lava gushes out through the crack in the earth, it cools and solidifies. This process is repeated over and over, so that a cone forms around the opening. It grows higher and higher and in the end becomes a mountain.

Sometimes a volcano keeps erupting and throwing out great clouds of smoke and ash and streams of frothy lava for many years at a time. Then, when enough of the internal gases have been released to ease the pressure far underground, the eruption stops. The lava inside the cone then cools and becomes solid, and plugs up the crack in the crust.

Over the years the pressure of the gases in the magma reservoir usually builds up again. And when it becomes

strong enough, it blows out the plug of solid lava, and once more the volcano erupts.

Once in a great while, the plug inside the volcano's mouth is so tight and firm and the pressure from within is so great that the entire mountain explodes. Katmai in Alaska blew up in this way in 1912. It created what is now known as the "Valley of Ten Thousand Smokes," an area where gas and smoke and clouds of steam issue from the ground through thousands of small vents in the earth's surface.

Some volcanoes never seem to stop erupting. Stromboli, a volcanic island off the coast of Italy, has been in constant eruption for more than 2,000 years. The twin volcanoes of Nyirangongo and Nyamlagira in the African Congo have been sending out lazy spirals of smoke ever since they were first discovered.

Mount Erebus, 800 miles from the South Pole, constantly belches columns of smoke and volcanic ash, although its sides are always covered with snow and ice. The Aleutian Islands, which extend across the Bering Sea from Alaska to Siberia, make up one of the most active volcanic regions in the world, even though they, too, almost always have a blanket of snow.

As far as we know, however, other volcanoes have become completely extinct. Among these are Fujiyama in Japan and Mount Shasta and Mount Hood in the United States.

The volcanic eruptions around the earth follow almost exactly the same pattern as earthquake disturbances. This is probably because both are basically caused by weak spots in the earth's crust.

Undersea Volcanoes

JUST AS earthquakes occur on the bottom of the ocean, so volcanoes frequently erupt on the sea floor. If they are vigorous enough, they form islands.

The island of Hawaii was created by five such undersea volcanoes. The five volcanic cones were so close together that they merged to form a single island. Together they constitute the highest volcanic mountain on earth, rising almost six miles above the sea bottom.

Every year dozens of volcanic islands raise their cones above the surface of the sea for a brief time, and then are washed away by the action of the waves and the wind.

One of the most dramatic examples of such an undersea volcano is Myojin, in the Pacific Ocean south of Japan. The crater of Myojin, which rises some 5,000 feet from the ocean bottom, now lies just under the Pacific's surface. For years it seemed as though it would become a permanent island.

In September 1952, the volcano began erupting, and the top of its cone emerged from the roiling waters. For several days it erupted and exploded continually, and at last blew itself up and disappeared. Then a Japanese research ship passed over the quiet water where it had been. Suddenly Myojin gave one violent upheaval and destroyed the ship and all on board.

Three months later, Myojin erupted again. This time it built an island about 100 feet high. The tiny island lasted from December until the following March, and then it, too, blew up and sank beneath the waves.

In April the volcano made its final eruption. Almost overnight it built up an island some 600 feet long and 150 feet high. This time, scientists thought, maybe Myojin is on the map to stay! But late that summer, when an American ship went out to see what progress the new island was making, Myojin had once more disappeared.

Geysers

GEYSERS might be described as small, harmless, and beautiful distant cousins of volcanoes, for they, too, are created by the earth's internal heat. Scientists still do not know all about a geyser's operation, but it is believed that one works something like this:

Water from the earth's surface penetrates deep down into long vertical cracks in the underlying rock which act as natural water pipes. The deeper the water goes, the greater the pressure upon it. And the greater the pressure, the higher the boiling point. The combination of pressure and heat turns the water at the bottom of the column into steam. The steam expands upward, pushing the water above it toward the surface. Finally the whole column of water and steam shoots up out of the "pipe" to produce a breathtaking fountain display.

There are three major areas in the world where geysers are known: Iceland, New Zealand, and Yellowstone National Park. The geysers of Yellowstone are the most spectacular.

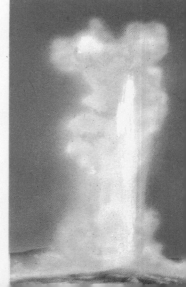

"Old Faithful" —
Yellowstone National Park

Pompeii

ON AUGUST 24, A.D. 79, the resort city of Pompeii lay basking on the shore of the Bay of Naples in the warm Mediterranean sun.

Behind the city, the lush, green slopes of Vesuvius towered into the sky. It was a beautiful mountain, and its fertile sides were covered with vineyards, orange groves, farms, and luxurious villas.

Suddenly, about noon, the ground under Pompeii began to shake violently, and a tremendous cloud of smoke, cinders, fire, and ashes spewed out of the mountain's top and showered down on the city. Within a few minutes, the entire population was buried alive under twenty to sixty feet of volcanic ashes and dust.

For nearly seventeen centuries Pompeii was forgotten. Then in 1748 a farmer who was digging a well unearthed some small statues, which he took to the authorities in Naples. The government became interested and took over the task of digging into the ruins.

The things that the search parties found, when they had succeeded in clearing out the ruins of Pompeii, were amazing. The mummified bodies of Roman soldiers were still at their sentry posts, exactly where they had been standing when the ashes had covered them. Entire families — parents, children, servants — were found huddled together in cellars where they had fled for protection. Food was still on tables, just as people had left it when they had fled in the middle of lunch.

Today Pompeii stands as an almost perfectly preserved relic of the life of the ancient Roman Empire.

Krakatao

PROBABLY THE loudest sound ever heard on earth was the explosion, in 1883, of the island of Krakatao in the Sunda Strait, between the Indian Ocean and the Java Sea.

Krakatao was a fairly large island, composed of three volcanic cones that rose more than 2,500 feet out of the sea. On August 26, 1883, the island exploded with a blast that was heard at Rodriguez Island, 3,000 miles away across the Indian Ocean, and in Ceylon, the Philippines, and Australia as well.

The eruption blew most of the island to bits and sank all but a small part of it beneath the sea. It created great tidal waves, which destroyed entire villages on the nearby islands of Java and Sumatra, in which nearly 40,000 people were drowned.

The fury of the blast threw great clouds of ashes and dust miles up into the air — so high that not all of it fell back to earth for more than two years. During this period, these dust clouds created orange, blue, green, and purple sunsets in almost every part of the world.

Mount Pelée

IN 1902, St. Pierre, on the island of Martinique in the West Indies, was a thriving city of 28,000 people. For several weeks, Mount Pelée, the volcanic mountain

that reared up behind the harbor, had been threatening to erupt. It was sending out clouds of smoke and ash and creating minor earthquakes.

The governor of Martinique appointed a committee of experts to investigate the mountain's activity. They reported that Mount Pelée was in no danger of a serious eruption — and the townspeople relaxed.

Then early on the morning of May 8, the mountain exploded in a series of tremendous blasts. A gigantic cloud of white-hot dust and gas — heated to more than 1,500 degrees — belched up out of the cone. Since it was heavier than the surrounding air, it rolled down the mountainside like a wave and completely enveloped the city.

In a matter of minutes — before anyone had a chance to escape — the whole town was on fire. All of the townspeople were suffocated or burned to death. All but two of the many ships in the harbor were destroyed instantly.

Of all the people in St. Pierre, only one man escaped with his life. He was Joseph Surtout, a prisoner who was in jail awaiting trial for murder. His prison cell had been so far underground that the flames and gases had not reached him. Four days after the eruption, a search party heard his feeble cries for help and saved him.

The ancestral seas are born

The Creation of the Seas

AS THE molten rock that formed the surface of the infant earth began to cool and solidify, gases bubbled up out of the seething interior and escaped into the cooler atmosphere that surrounded it. Here they collected together into great clouds of water vapor. When these clouds became dense enough, the moisture condensed and began to fall back to earth in the form of rain. But the earth's surface was still red-hot, so that as the raindrops approached it, they boiled away and returned into the upper atmosphere in the form of vapor.

And so, for probably millions of years, the earth was surrounded by a heavy blanket of rainclouds which was many miles thick. It was constantly condensing, falling as rain, and then being boiled back up into the upper reaches of the atmosphere.

Slowly, over these millions of years, the earth's crust hardened and cooled. It was a very long time before a raindrop could fall on the earth without fizzling away in a tiny vapor cloud. At last, when the surface rocks had cooled to the point where their heat could no longer boil water, the rain that had been collecting for many eons began to fall.

For hundreds, perhaps thousands, of years the rains came pouring down in an endless torrent. The water leveled off mountain ranges and cut great valleys in the earth. At last the huge deluge slowed and stopped, and the clouds overhead thinned out so that the sun could shine down upon the newborn earth. And now the deepest hollows of the earth's wrinkled and folded crust were filled with water. These were the ancestral seas.

The Oceans—Inner Space

TODAY we know less about the depths of the sea than we know about the planets of outer space. Astronomers have made fairly accurate maps of the moon and of Mars, but most of the floor of the sea is still uncharted.

Mount Everest, the tallest mountain on earth, is 29,000 feet high. But if placed in the deepest part of the Pacific, it would be covered by nearly two miles of water.

If all of the mountains and seas were leveled off into a perfectly round globe, our earth would be covered by water more than a mile and a half deep.

The geography of the sea floor

Why Sea Water Is Salty

EVER SINCE the first great rainfall which created the earth's seas, thousands of rivers have been flowing across the face of the land and carrying millions of tons of silt and sediment to the oceans each year. These dissolved materials include nearly all the minerals found in the earth, such as iron, gold, silver, calcium, and vast quantities of salt.

The heat of the sun evaporates some of the water on the seas' surface and sends it back up into the air in the form of water vapor. There it condenses into clouds and falls back to earth as rain and snow. This water then completes its endless cycle by flowing down to the sea again in the rivers, carrying more dissolved earth with it.

In the process of evaporation, the minerals are left behind in the oceans. Much of this material, such as iron and calcium, is absorbed by marine animals and plants and so are removed from the water. But the salts are not used by either the plants or the animals, and so they continue to accumulate in the sea in ever-increasing quantities. That is why sea water tastes salty, and will make you ill if you drink too much of it.

For many years chemists have been working on the problem of extracting from the waters of the sea such valuable elements as gold, silver, iron and magnesium. At some future time, they feel, sea water will be our most important source of these materials. They are also experimenting with ways to purify sea water so that it will be useful for irrigating desert lands.

The Geography of the Ocean Floor

IF ALL the waters of the sea were somehow drained away, the ocean floors would probably look not too unlike the bare contours of the dry land. You would see flat plains, deep canyons, valleys, hills, cliffs, and high mountain ranges. Sometimes the tops of these undersea mountains extend above the surface as islands, like Bermuda, the Azores, and the Hawaiian group.

The floor of the sea is dotted with extinct volcanoes whose tops have been leveled off by the ocean currents. Now and then these volcanoes spring into life and, as we have seen in an earlier chapter, create new islands.

In much the same way that rivers of water flow through the valleys of the land, rivers of mud and sand and silt flow through the valleys of the ocean floor. They flow so slowly that it is almost impossible to detect their movement, but they are constantly changing the geography of this vast underwater world.

Some submarine canyons and valleys seem to be extensions of river valleys that exist on land, such as the valleys of the Hudson River in the United States and the Congo River in Africa. Others appear to have no relation to land formations.

There are a number of deep rifts, or giant cracks in the sea bottom which are much longer, wider, and deeper than any canyons found on land. These were probably caused by a faulting of the earth's crust, which is considerably thinner at the bottom of the sea than it is anywhere else.

One such crack runs down the middle of the Atlantic Ocean. Some scientists think that this crack is growing wider and that lava is welling up from inside the earth to fill it. As a result, they believe that the continent of North America may be moving away from Europe at the rate of about one or two yards every 1,000 years.

The Currents of the Sea

THE WATER of the sea is constantly in motion — stirred up by the ebb and flow of the tides, the movement of the winds, its own differing densities, and the rotation of the earth. These sea currents travel in well-defined paths and in huge, concentric circles. They travel from ocean to ocean, and there is a complete mixing of the world's waters about once every 1,800 years.

If you pull the plug from a bathtub full of water, you

Sometimes the behavior of these currents is curious. Northwest of the West Indies and just south of Bermuda, there is an area in the Atlantic Ocean where the circling current of the Gulf Stream creates a center of dead calm. Seaweed is carried to this center by the current and cannot escape. As a result, the surface of this part of the sea resembles a floating island.

Some currents derive their motive power from the

The currents of the Atlantic   The currents of the Pacific

will notice that the water spirals down the drain in a clockwise motion — that is, from left to right. But if you were to do the same thing in Australia, you would find that the water spirals in just the *reverse* direction, or from right to left. This is a result of the rotation of the earth, which causes wind and water to veer to the *right* north of the equator, and to the *left* south of it.

In the same way, the ocean currents in the Northern Hemisphere circle from east to west, and those in the Southern Hemisphere from west to east.

Thus the currents that bring warm water up from the shores of tropical South America, by means of the Gulf Stream and the Atlantic Current, swirl north and east across the Atlantic and give a subtropical climate to the south of France, which is not much farther south than the border between the United States and Canada.

density of the water. Perhaps the most dramatic example of these are the currents that pass through the Strait of Gibraltar between the Atlantic Ocean and the Mediterranean Sea.

The weather around the Mediterranean is warm, and there is little rainfall. Therefore, the sea water that evaporates under the hot sun is not adequately replaced by rain or the flow of rivers. So it becomes saltier and denser. This heavy salt water sinks beneath the surface, creating a current that flows out through the strait and into the deep Atlantic.

To replace the water flowing out of the Mediterranean, water that is lighter and less salty flows in from the Atlantic. This means there are *two* currents, going in opposite directions through the same narrow stretch of water, with one passing over the other!

What Causes the Tides

ANYONE who has ever been to the seashore has seen the daily ebb and flow of the tides. At certain times of day, the level of the water rises, sometimes ten or fifteen feet. Then it recedes and leaves a long, empty stretch of beach behind it.

In ancient times people believed that tides were caused by the breathing of giant sea monsters. It was not until Sir Isaac Newton discovered the laws of gravity, in 1687,

water only about one foot. At the Bay of Fundy, just a few hundred miles north in Nova Scotia, the water level changes as much as forty feet.

For a long time scientists were puzzled by this peculiar behavior of the tides. Then they discovered that it was caused by irregularities in the depth and shape of the ocean floor.

We have seen that the sea floor is not flat. Instead, it

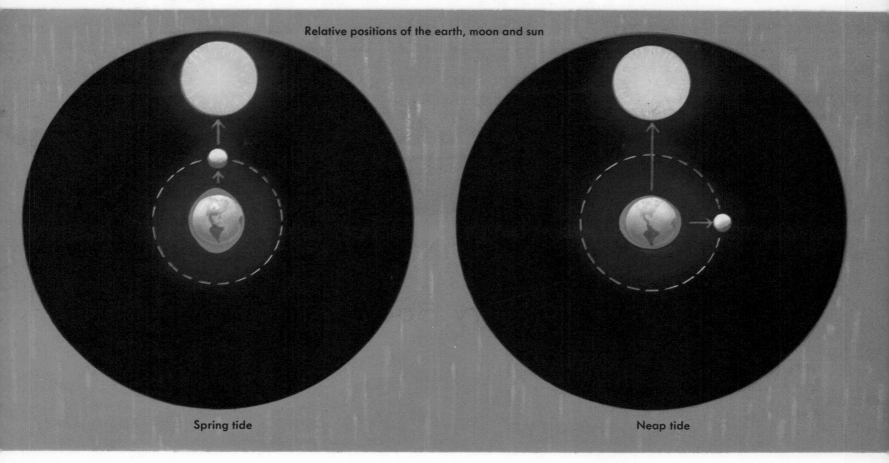

Relative positions of the earth, moon and sun

Spring tide

Neap tide

that the tides were found to be caused by the gravitational pull of the moon and, to a lesser degree, the sun.

During the periods of new moon and full moon, the sun, the earth, and the moon are all in a straight line. And so the moon and the sun work together to cause extremely high tides, known as *spring tides*. When the moon is in its first and third quarters, it is at right angles to the sun. Then the sun and moon tend to offset each other, which results in lower tides, called *neap tides*.

But there are many puzzling things about the movement of the tides that cannot be explained by the simple force of gravity.

Around most of the Atlantic, the tides come and go twice a day. But in parts of the Pacific, the tide comes in only once each day. At Nantucket Island off the coast of Massachusetts, high tide changes the level of the

is composed of huge basins, some broader and deeper than others. The water in these basins tends to move back and forth when it is disturbed, like the water in a bathtub or a dishpan. Water in a tub reacts more violently, however, than water in a shallow pan. Thus it is clear why the height of the tide depends upon the shape of the ocean basin as well as upon the pull of the moon and the sun.

One of the strangest tidal actions takes place at Mont-Saint-Michel, off the coast of Brittany in France. At high tide the castle is entirely surrounded by the sea. At low tide, however, the water recedes out of sight, and the castle is surrounded by a low, flat sand beach.

The "History Book" of Rocks

ONE DAY, about 500 million years ago, the strange-looking creature pictured above was swimming along through the warm waters of a primeval ocean. He was a *trilobite,* an ancient ancestor of crabs and lobsters, and although he was less than a foot long, he was one of the biggest animals then on earth.

When he lived, there was little or no life at all on the land; there was life only in the warm waters of the sea. And even in the sea there were no fish as we know them today. There were only crablike creatures like the trilobite — and worms, snails, jellyfishes, and sponges.

For some reason, on this day half a billion years ago, this particular trilobite died. His body sank to the silt and mud of the ocean floor, and the currents of the sea covered it up with still more mud and silt. As thousands and millions of years went by, the mud of the sea bottom slowly hardened into rock and layer piled up upon layer. The trilobite's body decayed and disappeared, but the complete and accurate outline of his form was preserved in the ageless rock.

Then, as we have seen in the chapter about the building of mountains, pressures from inside the earth slowly bent the rock in which the trilobite was encased, and lifted it out of the water. It rose at the rate of one or two inches every few hundred years, and at last it became the top of a mountain range. That is why scientists found the fossil remains of the long-dead trilobite, not on the floor of the sea into which it had sunk, but high up on the top of a mountain peak a thousand miles from the nearest ocean.

It is by studying the fossils of animals and plants which have been preserved for millions of years in layers of sedimentary rock, that we are able to learn about the life that existed on our planet when it was younger. The word "fossil" itself comes from the Latin *fossilis,* meaning "dug up."

The layers of fossil-bearing rock — composed for the most part of solidified mud and silt — have piled themselves one on top of the other over the ages. And so scientists have come to call them the "picture book" history of the earth. The oldest pages are at the bottom of the pile, and the youngest are at the top. Sometimes earthquakes and subterranean pressures break up the natural sequence — standing some of the pages on end and placing older ones above newer ones — but geologists have learned to tell them apart and to identify them correctly and place them in their proper time period.

Men have been observing fossils, and wondering about them, since the beginning of recorded history. The Greek geographer, Anaximander of Miletus, in the sixth century B.C., identified them as creatures that had once lived in the sea, but he was unable to explain how they had become embedded in rocks high on mountain tops.

In the Middle Ages, people thought that these creatures had been washed up on dry land by the waters of the Flood. Leonardo da Vinci, the great Italian painter and scholar who lived in the fifteenth century, proved his genius by correctly guessing that these fossil animals had been buried in the mud of ocean bottoms which had somehow hardened into rock and had been lifted out of the water to create mountains.

It remained, however, for an English engineer, William Smith — who made his original observations while supervising the construction of a canal — and two Frenchmen, Georges Cuvier and Alexandre Brongniart, in about the year 1800, to fit the pieces of the puzzle together so that scientists could accurately read this "history book" of the rocks.

By studying fossils — like those pictured on this page — we now know that the first life probably appeared on earth about two billion years ago in the form of a kind of *algae,* the green scum that we often see on the surface of ponds in the summertime.

Then, about five or six hundred million years ago, came the first primitive forms of animal life — such as worms, snails, and our friend, the trilobite. Following them came the fishes, the first animals with backbones. And then, something like two hundred million years ago, the first amphibians waddled out of the sea onto the land, developed lungs and legs, and became the ancestors of all air-breathing animals.

The slow, painstaking evolution of life went on — from the dinosaurs and other giant reptiles which once dominated the earth, to woolly mammoths and saber-toothed tigers, and finally to the primates who were the direct ancestors of modern man. And the whole story of the history of life is there for all to see in the "history book" of the rocks.

In the same way, we can also trace the development of plant life on the planet we live on — from algae and primitive seaweed, through ferns, palms, and the first fir trees to our modern trees and flowers.

STAGES OF ANIMAL EVOLUTION
AS SHOWN BY FOSSILS

PLEISTOCENE

BISON

MAN

PLIOCENE

PROCAMELUS

MIOCENE

SABER-TOOTHED TIGER

MOROPUS

OLIGOCENE

SUBHYRACODON

NOTHARCTUS

EOCENE

EOBASILEUS

PALEOCENE

PANTOLAMBDA

CENOZOIC ERA

PTERANODON

CRETACEOUS

TYRANNOSAURUS

BRONTOSAURUS

JURASSIC

ARCHAEOPTERYX

MESOZOIC ERA

PHYTOSAUR

TRIASSIC

SALTOPOSUCHUS

PERMIAN

CARBONIFEROUS

MEGANEURON

DEVONIAN

CROSSOPTERYGIAN

SILURIAN

COILED CEPHALOPOD

SCORPION

NAUTILOID

ORDOVICIAN

PALEOZOIC ERA

TRILOBITE

BRACHIOPOD

CAMBRIAN

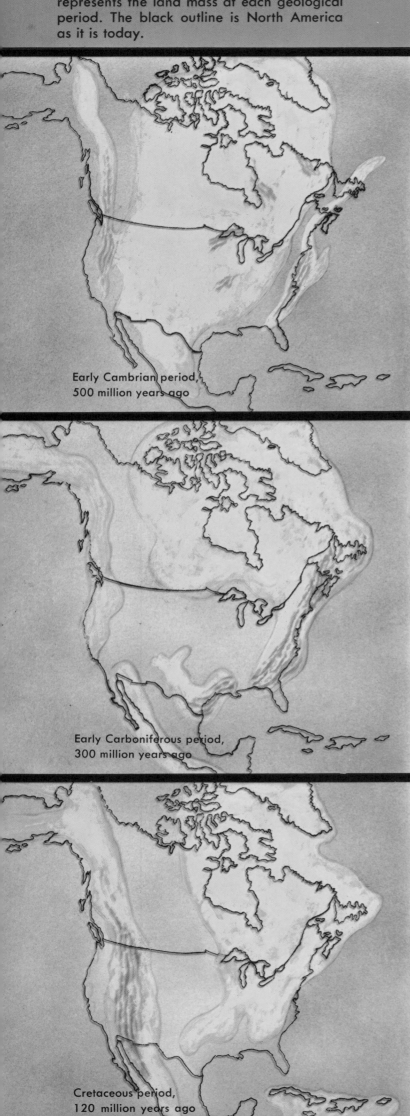

How the outline of the North American continent has changed over the ages. The yellow represents the land mass at each geological period. The black outline is North America as it is today.

Early Cambrian period, 500 million years ago

Early Carboniferous period, 300 million years ago

Cretaceous period, 120 million years ago

The Changing Earth

THE FACE of our planet is changing every day, just as it has been changing ever since the dawn of creation. Most of the time, the change is too slow for us to see — such as mountains that rise at the rate of a few inches every thousand years. But if we look closely, we can see evidences of this ever-present change all around us.

After a heavy rain the water of a stream is muddy. This means that the rain has washed soil away from one place and the stream is carrying it to another. Slowly but surely the hills through which the stream flows are being worn down and leveled off.

If you go to the seashore, you can see how the tumbling waves are constantly washing away the sands of the beach. After thousands and millions of years, the shorelines of the oceans are changed. Silt from inland streams, sand from the shore, and the bodies of countless billions of sea creatures that die every year and sink to the bottom, raise the level of the sea floor. As a result, the water of the oceans is being lifted ever higher.

So it would seem that one day, in the far distant future, what is now dry land will be completely covered by the sea. But we have seen that new land masses are constantly rising. And so we are pretty sure that at least a third of the earth's surface will probably always be dry land as it is now — although the shapes of the continents will no doubt keep on changing, as they have in the past.

Again, geologists can read the story of the changing continents in the "picture-history book" of the rocks.

Fossils of animals that once lived on land have been found at the bottom of the sea. This indicates that these particular sea bottoms were at one time a part of the land. And this seems reasonable since the tops of many mountains once lay on the bottom of the sea.

Obviously, nobody knows for sure what the earth was like a billion years ago. But a careful study of these fossil clues has given scientists the following picture of the face of the land at various periods of geologic history.

Half a billion years ago seas spread across the interior of the United States, on to the Pacific border and northward to the Arctic Ocean. One hundred and fifty million years later a similar pattern existed, although the eastern part of the United States was by then dry land. A hundred million years ago, as the age of dinosaurs drew to a close, a vast sea covered the western United States and Canada, much of Mexico and lapped over the southern and southeastern states. Thereafter the North American continent began to assume its present familiar shape.

Still, even as recently as the early Stone Age, only a few thousand years ago, the British Isles and the southern tip of Sweden were connected to the continent of Europe. A vast, swampy plain filled in what is now the North Sea and the English Channel. The Thames River in England and the Rhine River in Germany flowed together to create one mighty stream.

At this time, too, Siberia was probably connected to Alaska by a land bridge across the Bering Strait. It is believed that early man must have migrated across this bridge from Asia to become the ancestor of the American Indians. Mammoths, the huge, furry forerunners of elephants, apparently took this same route, for their fossilized bones have been found in American deserts.

The geologic history of what is now the City of New York furnishes a good example of how the face of the land changes.

The main part of New York City, Manhattan, is situated on a long, narrow island which, at its highest point, is only a few feet above sea level. It is a city of tall buildings, crowded streets and splendid parks, where many millions of people live and work.

But about 250 million years ago, New York was part of a chain of volcanic islands, with an ocean on one side and a vast inland sea on the other.

Then the rocks of the earth's crust folded, and the entire area was lifted out of the water to form a range of mountains. These were gradually worn down by the winds and the rains of more than a hundred million years — and new mountains rose to take their place, only to be worn down in turn.

Then glaciers came down from the polar icecap and cut New York into its present shape, grinding out the bed of the Hudson River on one side and Long Island Sound on the other.

When Henry Hudson first saw the island in 1609, the contours of Manhattan looked almost exactly as they do today — except that what was then a pleasant woodland is now the world's busiest city.

But like most other parts of the earth's surface, the land on which New York City now stands will some day very likely sink back into the sea from which it came. This fact, however, need not alarm us, for it will not happen for many more millions of years.

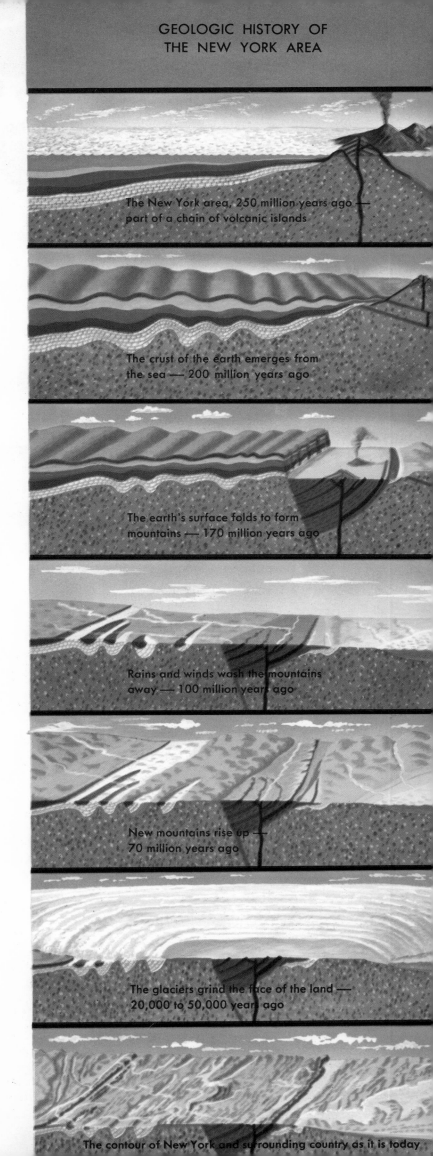

GEOLOGIC HISTORY OF THE NEW YORK AREA

The New York area, 250 million years ago — part of a chain of volcanic islands

The crust of the earth emerges from the sea — 200 million years ago

The earth's surface folds to form mountains — 170 million years ago

Rains and winds wash the mountains away — 100 million years ago

New mountains rise up — 70 million years ago

The glaciers grind the face of the land — 20,000 to 50,000 years ago

The contour of New York and surrounding country as it is today

A typical mountain glacier

The Rivers of Ice

A GLACIER is a river of ice which flows down a mountainside. Like a river of running water, it cuts out a stream bed for itself and transports vast amounts of rock and soil from the mountain's top and sides to the valley below. In fact, it may eventually remove an entire mountain or change the shape of a whole mountain range.

Glaciers are formed in high places where there is snow all the year round. As fresh snow falls and piles up on the snows of previous winters, the snowfield becomes deeper and heavier until the bottom layers are compressed into a sheet of solid ice.

When this huge mass of snow and ice gets thick and heavy enough, it breaks away and begins to flow down the mountain. New layers of snow and ice accumulate in the crevice made when the glacier tore itself from the mountain wall, and the river of ice is replenished.

You may wonder how a solid like ice can be said to flow. The answer is that when the bottom layer of ice is subjected to the great pressures exerted upon it by the top layers, it actually changes shape and flows, much like a plastic.

A glacier flows very slowly, usually only a few inches a day. When it passes through a narrow walled valley, it flows faster than when it is moving over a broader, less confined area. And the ice in the center moves more rapidly than the ice on either side. In these respects the glacier's flow resembles that of a stream of water.

The glacier continues downward until its lower edge reaches a point on the mountainside where the temperatures are warm enough to melt ice and snow in summer. There it begins to melt, and the water continues on in the form of streams and rivers.

As the glacier moves down the mountain, it plucks out large chunks of rock and carries them along with it. A great portion of the rocks is ground up by the tremendous pressure of the ice into a fine powder called *rock flour*. This powder gives the ice of the glacier, and the water that melts from its lower end, a blue-gray color like that of skim milk.

Glaciers are found in every part of the world where there are high, rugged mountains. Some of the most spectacular are in Alaska, the Canadian Rockies, the Alps, and the Himalayas. In Africa, glaciers lie on the slopes of Kilimanjaro and Mount Kenya, which stand almost squarely upon the equator. The jungles and farmlands on their lower slopes are fed in part by glacial waters.

Continental Glaciers

MOST OF Greenland and the Antarctic continent is covered by huge glaciers that are different from those which flow down the sides of the Andes or the Alps. These are *continental glaciers,* also sometimes called *ice sheets* or *icecaps.*

These ice sheets act like pancake batter when it is poured onto a griddle. The ice flows outward on all sides from the middle. When the edges reach the warmer waters of the ocean, they break off and float away as icebergs.

About ten per cent of the earth's land surface, nearly six million square miles, is covered by glaciers. Most of this vast area, of course, consists of the ice sheets of Greenland and Antarctica. The mountain glaciers make up only a small part of the total.

It is impossible to make an accurate estimate of the amount of water locked up in these glaciers, mainly because we have no way of knowing the exact thickness of the Antarctic icecap. But estimates range from about two-and-a-half to six million cubic miles. If all this ice were somehow to melt away, it would raise the present level of the seas between 65 and 200 feet! This would put most of our present coastlines under water.

The Great Ice Age

THOUSANDS of years ago, a series of glaciers spread southward from the North Pole and buried more than one fourth of the earth's land surface under a crushing sheet of ice.

The ice covered all of Canada, all of New England and New York, the entire Great Lakes area, and many parts of the western plains. As the great glaciers slowly advanced, they eroded mountains, changed the courses of old rivers and created new ones, gouged out the Great Lakes basin, and filled the lakes with water as the ice melted and the glaciers receded.

They left behind them thousands of new lakes, hills and valleys, and the rock-strewn landscape of New England, which marked their lower edge.

Today most of the glaciers in the world are still receding, and this process has greatly speeded up in the last few years. As recently as fifty years ago, resort hotels were built in some parts of the Alps to give tourists a fine view of a particular glacier. Today many of these glaciers have receded completely out of sight.

Iceberg breaking off from continental glacier

The farthest advance of the Ice Age in North America

The Wonderful Cycle of Water

AS FAR as we know for sure, our earth is the only planet in the universe on which there is water. We know that life originated in the sea, and that all life, both plant and animal, depends upon water for its survival.

Except for a very small amount of water that volcanoes bring to the surface from deep inside the earth, all of our water comes from the ocean — and then ultimately returns to it. It is this wonderful cycle of water that sustains the miracle of life.

Under the sun's hot rays, a certain amount of sea water evaporates each day and ascends into the air in the form of water vapor. There it condenses into clouds which float in over the land. And then, as drops of rain or flakes of snow, it falls back on the earth. It has been estimated that every second of every day about 16 million gallons of water pour down out of the sky — because somewhere in the world it is always raining.

This rain water or melted snow follows four main paths in the completion of the water cycle.

1. A large part of it evaporates back into the air when the rain stops and the sun comes out.

2. Some of it is soaked up by the roots of growing plants and then "breathed" back into the atmosphere by the plants' leaves.

3. Some penetrates into the ground to form the underground reservoirs that we tap when we dig a well.

4. The rest runs off the land by means of streams and rivers and returns again to the sea.

The Rivers

RIVERS have their beginnings on the sides of hills and mountains, which are known as *watersheds*. The story of a typical river might go something like this:

A heavy rain falls on a hillside, and water drips from the leaves of the trees to the ground. There it collects into little rills which cascade down the slope. As these tiny streams flow down the hill, a number of them merge together to form a larger one. And this, too, merges with others, until at last they become a small brook.

By the time the water reaches the valley that lies between the hills, hundreds — perhaps thousands — of these little rills and rivulets have flowed together to make a broad river. Now the current slows down, and the river becomes comparatively leisurely and unhurried.

Ever since the water started running down the hill, it has been carrying pebbles and bits of soil along with it. As the river slows down, it may leave some of the heavier parts of this load along the way. These deposits of stones and silt often create an obstruction on one side of the riverbed, causing the current to swerve to the opposite bank, which it tends to scoop out. In turn, this scooped-out bank sends the current back to the other side. The result is a series of curves, or *meanders,* that make the river wind from side to side.

These meanders greatly increase the distance that a stream covers from its source to its mouth. Many rivers flow as much as twenty-five or thirty miles to cover five miles as the crow flies.

A great river like the Mississippi pours billions of gallons of water a day back into the sea. This water contains millions of tons of mud and silt which the river has been carrying out of the land over which it has flowed.

When the current of the river hits the heavier, quieter water of the sea, it is quickly slowed down. As a result, vast amounts of this mud and silt settle to the bottom at the river's mouth to create a wide, flat area of extremely fertile land known as a *delta.*

The deltas of the Mississippi and the Nile, in particular, are famous for the rich farmlands that they have built up over the centuries. In fact, most of the country that is now the Netherlands was created by deltas of the Rhine and other rivers that flowed from the German highlands down to the North Sea.

For the most part, the march of civilization has followed the course of the world's great rivers. The valleys of the Nile, the Tigris, and the Euphrates were the birthplaces of modern man. The great cities of Europe were built along the Danube, the Rhine, the Elbe, and the Seine. And the westward progress of America followed the Ohio, the Tennessee, the Mississippi, the Missouri, and the Columbia.

There are two chief reasons why this has been so. In the first place, the river valleys were generally the most fertile parts of the land. Secondly, rivers offered an easy means of transportation from one community to the other.

The ten longest rivers in the world are:

The Nile (Africa)	4,053 miles
The Mississippi-Missouri (N. America)	3,986 miles
The Amazon (S. America)	3,900 miles
The Yangtze (Asia)	3,100 miles
The Congo (Africa)	2,900 miles
The Hwang Ho (Asia)	2,700 miles
The Amur (Asia)	2,700 miles
The Lena (Asia)	2,645 miles
The Mekong (Asia)	2,600 miles
The Niger (Africa)	2,600 miles

A flash flood on a desert in the western United States

The Rampaging Rivers

NATURE has a wonderful way of keeping the cycle of water in good order. In the springtime, when farmlands need a lot of water for the coming crops, seasonal rains (we call them April showers) plus the melting of the winter snows keep the rivers full. During the hot months of midsummer, when rainfall is generally light, small streams dwindle down until often there is barely an inch or two of water dribbling over the rocks of the creek bed. Then the streams are replenished by the rains of autumn.

But sometimes it does not rain according to schedule. Rains may be so unusually heavy that the normal river-banks cannot contain them. Then the rivers overflow into the surrounding land and create a flood.

Floods can be terribly destructive. They wash away fertile topsoil and may leave the land unfit for cultivation for years to follow. They are dread destroyers of property, sometimes washing away entire towns and taking a horrible toll of human lives.

The Hwang Ho, or Yellow River, is called "China's sorrow" because it has probably had the worst flood history of any river on earth. Since ancient times it has overflowed at nearly regular intervals, and these recurring floods have repeatedly changed its course. The worst flooding of the Hwang Ho took place in 1887, when more than 30,000 square miles of land were inundated and seven million people were drowned.

Since the Mississippi River system drains nearly one third of the United States, it is easy to see why excessive rains make it rise to flood level. Its floods have often devastated large areas in the valleys of the Ohio and the Missouri and the main valley of the Mississippi itself. They have frequently raised the height of the water by more than fifty feet and swept away homes and farmlands as the rampaging river rushed toward the Gulf of Mexico, sometimes carrying whole towns along with it.

The famous Johnstown Flood in 1889 was caused when a weakened dam across the South Fork River was overflowing with water from rain-swollen Lake Cone-maugh. It burst without warning and sent an overpowering wall of water crashing down onto the unsuspecting town. Many of the townspeople were able to escape at the last minute into the surrounding Pennsylvania hills, but the flood waters almost destroyed the entire city and wiped out more than two thousand lives.

A peculiar kind of flood occurs in the desert. For possibly three hundred days out of the year, the sandy, rocky land is dry and arid. Suddenly storm clouds gather and the sky opens up and sends a deluge down to drench the parched earth.

Flood Control

The rain water, which falls on the sun-baked earth in great quantities and in a very short time, rushes down the gullies and arroyos in a great wall of water which carries everything before it. Then, in a few hours, it is gone, having been greedily sucked up by the thirsty sand.

These desert floods are known as *flash floods* because they give no warning of their approach. For this reason, an experienced desert traveler will never camp in what he knows to be a dry stream bed. He is aware that a flash flood is likely to come roaring down the gully unexpectedly and sweep away both him and his camp before he has a chance to get out of his sleeping bag.

Some floods, however, have beneficial, instead of destructive results — like the annual flooding of the Nile River in Egypt.

Each spring, the torrential rains of the central African jungles pour into the headwaters of the Nile and cause it to overflow the banks of its lower valley. This great volume of water spreads out over the desert and leaves there a rich deposit of loam and silt, which have been washed down from the mountains of the interior.

In this fertile coating of soil, the Egyptians grow their crops of cotton, fruit, and grain. Then, after a year has passed — after the crops have been harvested and the land has been baked dry by the desert sun — the floods return to make the land rich and fertile once more.

ONCE a flood has started, there is nothing men can do to stop it. The only cure is prevention.

This has been done most effectively by building dams which not only hold the floods in check but release the waters in controlled quantities. Often river channels are straightened, widened, and deepened, so that rising water will stay within the river beds instead of spreading out over the surrounding countryside.

One of the most effective methods of flood control has been to undo the damage that man himself has done to the land.

When America was first settled, the hills were covered with thick forests. The tree roots not only drank up the rain water as it fell, but also acted as millions of small dams and held back its headlong rush down the slopes to the rivers. But when the pioneers cleared away the trees for timber and made the land into planted fields, there was little to stop torrents of rain water from pouring down hillsides in a fury. And not only did the water escape in vast quantities, but it washed along with it many millions of tons of valuable topsoil.

Today one of the major flood-control projects of the United States Department of Conservation is the reforestation of highlands at the headwaters of major rivers, so that Mother Nature will once again be able to do her share in the prevention of floods.

Lakes and Swamps

WE HAVE seen how the world's water makes its endless cycle — from the sea, to the clouds, down to earth as rain, through the rivers, and back to the sea again. But some of this water is inevitably detoured on its journey and trapped for a time in natural depressions in the earth's surface where it becomes part of a lake.

It is probable that most lake basins were created by the action of ancient glaciers. As these great ice masses moved over the land, they scooped out hollows in the earth — or widened and deepened those that already

Sometimes landslides or lava flows dam up a stream and cause a lake to be born. Other lakes, like Crater Lake in Oregon, lie in the craters of long-dead volcanoes.

In places, an upheaval of a land mass long ago cut off a section of the sea. Lake Onego in Siberia was at one time part of the Arctic Ocean, and Lake Nicaragua in Central America was a gulf of the Pacific. One of the loveliest lakes in the world, Lake Geneva in Switzerland, is a glacier-deepened place in the valley of the Rhône River.

Lake Patzcuaro, Mexico

existed — which were then filled up by rivers that the melting ice created. More than half of all the lakes in the world are located in Canada and the northern part of the United States, and they are mostly the result of scars made on the land during the Great Ice Age.

Lake basins, however, are made by other means as well.

When the mountains were being built, the earth's crust was distorted and twisted out of shape, so that a great many lake beds were formed. The Great Salt Lake in Utah and the lakes that lie inside Africa's Great Rift were created by such movements of the earth's crust.

Lakes are fed by rivers and also drained by them. Where this two-way system of intake and outgo is working, the water of the lake is as unsalty as that of the rivers, and it is known as a *fresh-water lake*. But when there is no outlet from the lake, the water becomes salty.

The Caspian Sea in Asia Minor, the largest lake in the world, is a salt-water lake — as are the Dead Sea in Palestine and the Great Salt Lake.

The water of the Dead Sea is more than seven times saltier than ocean water. It actually contains 26 per cent salt, by volume, and is so dense and briny that no plant or animal life can exist in it. That, of course, is how it got its name.

The water of Great Salt Lake is a little over 20 per cent salt and is so dense that a human body cannot sink. The Caspian Sea, on the other hand, is only 1.3 per cent salt, about halfway between fresh water and ocean water.

The largest of the fresh-water lakes is Lake Superior on the U.S.-Canadian border. It is 350 miles long and 160 miles wide. Second in size is Lake Victoria in Africa.

Lake Titicaca in South America is the highest navigable lake in the world. It lies at an altitude of 12,644 feet on top of the Andes Mountains. The lowest-lying lake is the Dead Sea — 1,292 feet below sea level.

As soon as a lake basin is formed, the feeding rivers begin to deposit large quantities of silt and sediment on its bottom. Over a long period of time, these deposits fill the lake completely, turning it first into a swamp, and then a meadow. The last of its water runs off in the form of rivers and continues on its journey to the sea.

Lake Chad, in Africa, is already more of a swamp than a true lake. It will probably not be too many years before all of its water dries up and disappears, and it will be only a vast area of soggy ground. Then this, too, will eventually dry up, and Lake Chad will become part of the Sahara desert. Many inland swamps have been created by the drying-up of lakes.

Lakes, as a whole, are the least permanent features of the planet we live on. Even at the moment they are born, they begin to dry up. All lakes, including the largest ones, are undergoing this continuous drying-up process. Lake Superior, for example, is only a remnant of a much larger lake. Great Salt Lake was once a fresh-water lake 1,000 feet deep, but today its mean depth varies between 15 and 25 feet. Death Valley in California is the bed of a long-lost lake.

Strangely enough, the rivers that feed lakes and fill them up are also the means of eventually destroying them.

The greatest expanse of true swampland in the world, the Florida Everglades, are the remains of what was once the ocean floor. The land rose up, and the line of the sea retreated. Now the Everglades are gradually going dry. Parts of them have been drained by artificial means to provide farmlands and townsites — but by doing this, man has only helped speed up Nature's process. Streams have already begun to form in the Everglades, and eventually they will accomplish the same purpose as the man-made drainage ditches. One day the entire Everglades will be rich, fertile farming country.

RAIN →

ZONE OF AERATION

WATER TABLE

PERMEABLE SANDSTONE

ZONE OF SATURATION

IMPERMEABLE SHALE

Water Under the Ground

WHENEVER we dig a well to supply water to our homes, we are tapping a vast reservoir that lies unseen deep in the ground. Indeed, there is much more water under the ground than there is in all the surface lakes and ponds.

Every time it rains, a certain amount of rain water is soaked up by the earth. Some of it is held in suspension by the soil and feeds the roots of growing plants. But most of it seeps down to a level where all the cracks and openings in the underlying rocks are completely filled with water.

This level is called the *water table,* and the reservoir of underground water extends down from it to the layers of solid rock through which water cannot penetrate. Between the water table and the solid rock, the water flows. But since it has to move through cracks and openings in the rock, its flow is much slower than that of water in a surface stream. The rate of flow in a river on the surface is measured in feet-per-second. But that of underground water is measured by feet-per-day or, in some places, feet-per-year.

When a well is dug deep enough to penetrate the water table, the water in the cracks and crevices quickly fills the hole and can be pumped out. As water is taken from the well, more water flows in to bring the level of the well back up to the level of the water table.

Generally the water table tends to follow the contours of the earth's surface. For this reason, it is possible to get water from a well drilled on the top of a hill, as well as from one drilled in the valley below.

Springs

WHEN the water table comes into contact with the ground surface — usually on the side of a hill — underground water seeps out to create a spring. Spring water is cooler and usually tastes sweeter than river water because it has not been exposed to the heat of the sun.

In some springs — one of the most famous is at Saratoga Springs, New York — the underground water picks up salt, sulphur, and other minerals as it seeps through the underlying rocks. This gives it a distinctive "mineral water" taste, which many people consider healthful.

Certain other springs — such as those at Hot Springs, Arkansas, and Warm Springs, Georgia — yield water that is considerably warmer than normal water. Some of this spring water gets its heat from masses of magma, or molten rock, that have worked their way close to the surface. In other springs the water is warm because it has flowed through cracks deep enough inside the earth to be affected by the earth's internal heat.

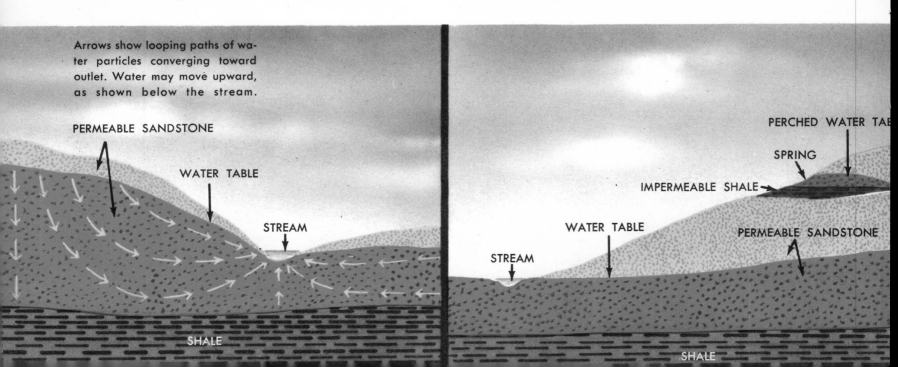

Arrows show looping paths of water particles converging toward outlet. Water may move upward, as shown below the stream.

PERMEABLE SANDSTONE

WATER TABLE

STREAM

SHALE

PERCHED WATER TABLE

SPRING

IMPERMEABLE SHALE →

WATER TABLE

PERMEABLE SANDSTONE

STREAM

SHALE

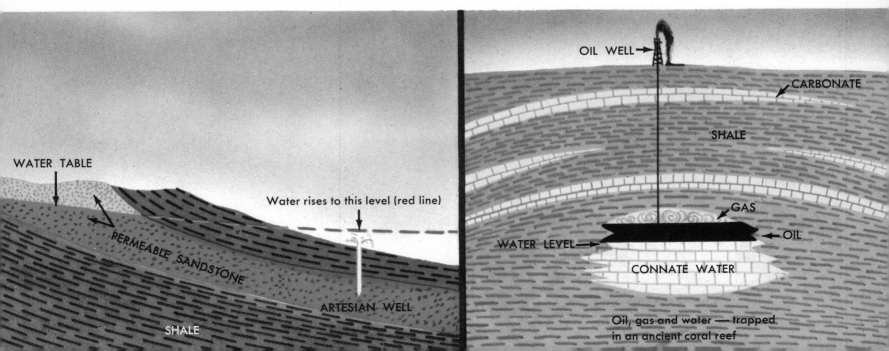

In ancient times, before the principle of underground water was understood, springs were thought to be the special work of the gods. When a spring suddenly erupted from the ground where there had been no water before, temples and shrines were often built around it.

The Bible tells of Moses tapping a rock and water gushing forth. Since Moses had been a shepherd for many years in the wilderness before he led the Children of Israel out of Egypt, he probably knew the best places to look for springs in dry, hilly country.

Occasionally a body of underground water is trapped above the main water table. This happens when a layer of solid rock, or other material through which water cannot seep, lies between it and the principal underground flow. This is called a "perched" water body and is usually found high on the top of a hill. The water escaping from its edge creates a hillside spring.

Artesian Flows

SOMETIMES a layer of water-bearing rock is encased in a layer of solid rock above as well as below. It thus becomes a sort of natural water pipe from which the water inside cannot escape. This is called an artesian flow.

If a well is drilled down to tap this imprisoned water supply, the pressure from either side will force the water to the surface. If there is a natural fissure in the earth and if the pressure is great enough, the water will gush up like a fountain.

Often the water in artesian streams flows hundreds of miles from the place where it descends into the earth as rain to the point where it emerges again from a well. For this reason, since they are not dependent upon local rainfall, artesian wells usually supply a reliable amount of water, even in times of extreme drought when other wells in the vicinity go dry.

Connate Water

MOST UNDERGROUND water, as we know, comes from rain and melted snow that seep into the earth. But there is still another kind, called connate water, which has lain sealed up in pockets of rock deep within the earth for many millions of years.

When the sedimentary rock formations were first formed on the bottom of the ancient seas, a certain amount of sea water was trapped inside them. Then the sea floors rose up and became part of the land, and the trapped water deposits rose with them.

A good example of connate water is the salt water that is brought up from deep oil wells. This water, while salty, is not like modern sea water. Perhaps the waters of ancient seas were different from today's sea water, or perhaps the old sea water changed its chemical content during its long burial.

WATER TABLE

Water rises to this level (red line)

PERMEABLE SANDSTONE

ARTESIAN WELL

SHALE

OIL WELL

CARBONATE

SHALE

GAS

WATER LEVEL

OIL

CONNATE WATER

Oil, gas and water — trapped in an ancient coral reef

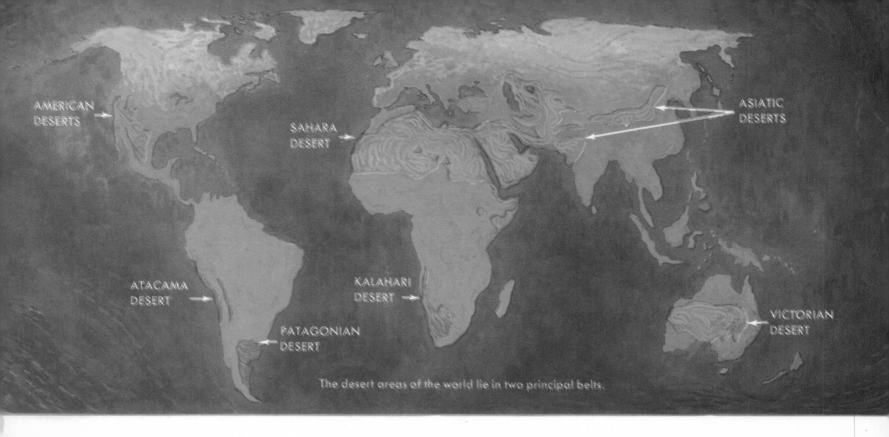

The desert areas of the world lie in two principal belts.

The Desert Wastes

AS YOU can see on the map above, the dry, bare nearly waterless areas of the world that we call deserts are distributed around the globe in two fairly well-defined bands. Between them are the lush, green jungles of the rainy lands that lie close to the equator. On either side, to the north and south, are the temperate zones.

Deserts are the result of a lack of rainfall, and the dryness of desert climates is caused by the peculiar behavior of winds in these parts of the globe.

Deserts closest to the equator are formed because they lie in a belt in which an excess amount of air has been piled up. Therefore the air begins to descend and to spread out both north and south along the surface. As the air descends, it becomes warmer. Because it is warmer, it can hold more moisture. So the desert winds are not only hot, but they drink up whatever moisture there is. It is almost impossible for Nature to squeeze this water out of the air and produce rain.

However, as the air keeps moving toward the equator, it becomes hotter and hotter, and thus begins to rise. When it has risen high enough into the cold reaches of the atmosphere, it quickly cools and suddenly releases its accumulated moisture in the torrential rains that drench the heavy jungles of the equatorial belt.

The Sahara Desert in North Africa, the Kalahari Desert in South Africa, the Arabian Desert, the great Victorian Desert which covers most of Australia, and the Sonora Desert in our Southwest were created in this way.

Some deserts, however, came about because an area was hemmed in by high mountain ranges which cut off the rain-carrying winds. The desert lands of Nevada, Utah, and Colorado were caused by the fact that the Sierra Nevada Mountains rise up abruptly on the western edge, thus diverting the moisture-bearing breezes that blow in from the Pacific.

The Face of the Desert

WHEN WE look out over the desert, it seems devoid of life. Except for a few shriveled shrubs and cactus spines, there is almost no vegetation on the sandy, rocky ground. In places, the fierce, dry wind has blown the rocks bare of sand and soil—and has cut the rocks themselves into weird twisted patterns, so that the landscape looks like the naked, lifeless surface of the moon.

By day the hot, fiery ball of the sun beats down out of the clear, cloudless sky so fiercely that a man could not survive for more than an hour or two without shade. Then, when the sun sinks at last behind the desert's rim, the temperature may drop so suddenly and so low that an unprotected traveler might freeze to death before the first light of morning.

It rarely rains in the desert, and when it does, the rainfall is usually scanty and short-lived. But sometimes a cloudburst cascades without warning from the sky. When this happens, the dry ground, baked brick-hard by the sun, sheds the water, which immediately races down gullies and arroyos to create the desert's fearsome flash floods.

Such a flash flood may rage for only a few minutes. And there is nowhere for this furious river of rain water to go, so it gradually spreads out over the land and is quickly drunk up by the thirsty earth. The desert plants greedily hoard the moisture in their long root systems, so that it will continue to nourish them during the long, hot, dry spell that is sure to follow.

The seeds of some desert plants lie dormant in the dry earth for months, and even years, at a time. Then the magic of the rain touches them, and overnight they burst into glorious life, briefly covering the entire desert with a brilliant coat of many colors. Then, just as quickly as they bloomed, they wither and die, waiting patiently for the next rain to restore them to life again.

Very few rivers flow through the desert, for the dry soil would soak up their water long before it could be carried to the sea. The only exceptions are rivers like the Colorado and the Nile, which originate in high mountainous country where plentiful rainfall and melting snows assure them of a boundless water supply at their source.

The Oasis

THERE is very little ground water under a desert. As we know, ground water depends upon regular rainfall to replenish itself, and the stingy rainfall of the desert is soon soaked up by the surface soil and evaporated back into the hot, dry air.

Now and then an artesian flow, which may bring water from rainy areas hundreds or even thousands of miles away, emerges on the surface of the desert as a spring. Such a spring creates an oasis, and these isolated garden spots—with their fruit trees, flowers, grass, and palms—glisten like green jewels in the midst of the brown, forbidding wasteland.

In the Sahara all of the towns are built around such oases, and the few roads that cross the desert go from one oasis to the next.

As lifeless and hostile as they seem, desert lands are becoming increasingly important to modern man.

The ancient Egyptians used the water of the Nile to irrigate the surrounding desert. By means of irrigation, the Mormon settlers turned the desert of Utah into productive farming country. And California's Imperial Valley, which only a few years ago was an empty and barren waste, is today one of the world's richest farmlands.

The Great American Desert

The Sculpture by Wind and Water

A STRONG breeze blowing against a hillside — a stream meandering through a pleasant valley — a line of whitecaps rolling in on a shoreline and dissolving in clouds of white spray as they break against the rocks.

As you look at these, they seem to be the most peaceful and ineffectual acts of nature. And yet wind and water are constantly at work, reshaping the surface of the earth, wearing it away, trying to level it off.

As breakers pound against a rocky shore, they pick up stones and grains of sand, which they hurl against the face of a cliff. Gradually the softer parts of the rock wear

gish. But when water runs swiftly, its destructive work is more dramatic and can be plainly seen.

The water that roars over the brink of Niagara hits the bottom of the pool below the falls with a tremendous impact. As a result, the pool is constantly being widened and deepened, and the swirling, rolling water cuts back under the face of the falls, weakening and cracking its foundation.

Not so very long ago, a whole section of the falls collapsed and tumbled into the river. It has happened many times in the past, and it will continue to happen, until

The Green Bridge of Wales, a sea-carved formation on the Welsh coast

away, sometimes forming such weirdly shaped structures as the arches and spires shown here.

In other places, the ocean waves change the shoreline by building it up, instead of tearing it down. Where beaches are long and sloping and waves are gentle, the incoming water carries sand from the sea bottom and deposits it on the beach. And year by year the beach grows higher and broader. Daytona Beach in Florida, where the sand is so firm and hard and the beach is so wide that it is used as an automobile race track, was built up in this way.

We know that running water is constantly changing the beds of rivers, even those that seem to be most slug-

Niagara Falls is many miles upstream from where it is now.

Perhaps the most breathtaking examples of the manner in which wind and water sculpture the face of the land can be found in our American West, where odd rock formations are a wondrous scenic attraction.

The strange monuments and cathedral-like formations pictured here are in Bryce Canyon National Park in Utah.

At one time this was a broad, sandy plain. But as millions of years went by, the rivulets that flowed across it dissolved the limestone in the underlying rock and ate away the harder rocks bit by tiny bit, until Bryce Canyon became the place of fairyland palaces that it is today.

Bryce Canyon, Utah

The action of the wind is not nearly as important as that of water in the reshaping of the land. Oddly enough, it is not the violent winds, like cyclones and tornadoes, that have the most telling effect. These storms blow up and die down too quickly. Instead, the more moderate winds, which blow steadily year after year, are the true sculptors of Nature.

We have seen how in desert regions the wind blows away the sand and shifts it from place to place, often leaving outcroppings of bare rock. Then the wind-blown sand is blasted against the rock with the same effect that sandpaper has when you rub it across a piece of wood.

Gradually the rock is worn away, the softer parts going first and the harder parts remaining.

The sand dunes of the desert and the seashore provide a classic example of the work of the wind. Steady breezes blow the tiny particles of sand before them over earth that is almost barren of vegetation, and the dunes pile up and change their shapes and move from place to place.

The wind plays strange tricks with dunes, forming some of them into the shape of a crescent and others into the pattern of ocean waves. But always the dunes keep shifting and changing position before the force of the wind, so that the landscape changes from day to day.

A natural bridge

A wind-blasted balanced rock

GNEISS

GRANITE

RED SANDSTONE

FOSSILIFEROUS LIMESTONE

RED SHALE

Rocks and Stones

BASICALLY three kinds of rock make up the crust of the planet we live on. They are *igneous* rocks, *sedimentary* rocks, and *metamorphic* rocks.

Igneous (meaning "fire") rocks form when molten magma cools and solidifies. The first rocks to form were igneous rocks, when the outer portion of the infant earth began to cool. And they have been forming ever since, either deep within the earth's crust, or at its surface when lava spreads from volcanic centers.

Igneous rocks vary greatly in composition and appearance, since they may be composed of many different combinations of minerals. The two commonest and most important igneous rocks are *basalt* and *granite*.

Basalt, sometimes called traprock, is the stone that is usually crushed to make surfaces for roads and driveways. It varies in color from gray to black.

Granite is one of the most widely used building stones because of its strength and endurance. Its color ranges from white to gray to green to pink to red. It has been quarried and used commercially since the time of the ancient Egyptians.

The Pharaohs of Egypt used granite for their statues, obelisks, palaces, and temples — just as we use it today for the construction of modern buildings, monuments, and memorials.

Granite is found over much of the United States, although the most important commercial quarries are in the New England area.

Sedimentary rocks are composed of what, many millions of years ago, were layers of sand, gravel, and mud lying on the bottom of ancient seas. The individual particles were cemented together by minerals or hardened into rock under the great weight of the mud and sea water pressing down upon them. And so sedimentary rocks were slowly formed, layer upon layer.

Sedimentary rocks are found in a wide variety of brilliant colors. In the canyon country of the American West, they have all the bright hues of the rainbow — deep shades and delicate tints of yellow, red, orange, blue, purple, brown, buff, gray, green, and pink.

The most common sedimentary rocks are *sandstone, limestone,* and *shale*. While not as enduring as granite, sandstone and limestone are also widely used in building — and they are much easier to quarry. The White House in Washington is made of sandstone, painted white.

Limestone, quarried from cliffs along the upper Nile and floated down river on barges, was used to build the Great Pyramids of Egypt. It is still a common building material, but today its most important use is in industry. Limestone is powdered to make industrial cement, and

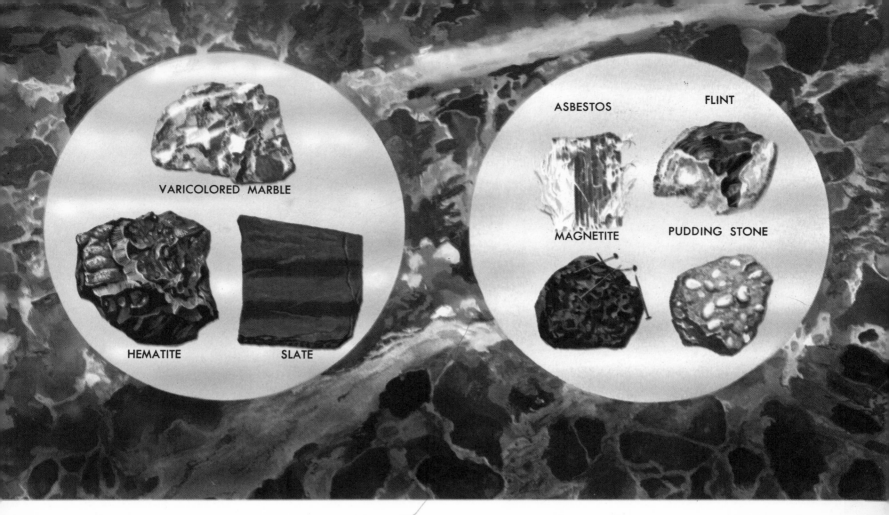

VARICOLORED MARBLE

HEMATITE

SLATE

ASBESTOS

FLINT

MAGNETITE

PUDDING STONE

it is crushed and mixed with iron ore in the manufacture of steel.

Metamorphic (meaning "made over") rocks are those that at one time were either igneous or sedimentary — but that were changed into a different form by such forces as heat and pressure from deep within the earth.

The metamorphic rocks that you most frequently see are *marble, slate,* and *quartzite.*

Marble, one of the most beautiful of all stones, was "made over" from limestone, a sedimentary rock. It can be white, black, green, red, or a combination of many colors streaked together.

The great masterpieces of early Italian and Greek sculpture were carved from marble, as are many of our statues and memorials today. Marble is also a favorite building material, especially where beauty is an important factor. The Capitol and the Lincoln Memorial, as well as many other government buildings in Washington, are made of American marble.

Slate, another important type of rock used in building, was "made over" from layers of compressed shale. The better grades of slate split easily into thin, uniform sheets with a smooth, even surface. Its major use is roofing for houses. When you consider that the slate on a roof is stone that has lain buried in the earth for millions of years, it is easy to understand why no amount of weathering by rain or snow can cause a slate roof to wear out.

Quartzite looks a great deal like sandstone, from which it was "made over." Quartzite is among the toughest of rocks. An outcropping of quartzite often takes the form of a cliff, from which the soil and softer rocks have eroded away.

Here are some unusual kinds of rocks.

ASBESTOS is a mineral found in metamorphic rocks in the form of long, silky fibers. These fibers can be woven into a fireproof cloth that is used to make brake linings and firefighting suits.

FLINT, a form of quartz, was used by the American Indians to make hatchets, knives, and arrowheads.

MAGNETITE, commonly called lodestone, is a special kind of heavy black rock containing a high percentage of iron ore. It is a natural magnet and will pick up pins, needles, and bits of metal. Christopher Columbus used a sliver of lodestone in the crude compass with which he plotted his course to the New World. And the log of his journey notes that he carried a spare in case his original needle somehow lost its magic quality of always pointing to the North Pole.

PUDDING STONE. Geologists call this rock a conglomerate. It is a form of sedimentary rock in which small pebbles, rock fragments, sand, and various rock-forming minerals have all been mixed, like the ingredients of a pudding, and cemented together in a solid mass. The process took many thousands of years.

Minerals — Rare and Common

IN GENERAL, a mineral may be defined as any solid element or compound formed by Nature's inorganic processes.

When the young earth changed from a swirling ball of cosmic dust into a molten sphere, it consisted largely of the eight basic elements that we know today — oxygen, silicon, iron, magnesium, sodium, aluminum, potassium, and calcium. Then, as the molten mass cooled and hardened, the elements combined with each other in many different patterns, to become the minerals with which we are familiar and which we use every day.

For example, common table salt is composed of sodium and chlorine. A diamond is formed from carbon, which is also the basic ingredient of coal. Rubies and sapphires come from corundum, which in another form is the rough, black rock used to make grindstones.

Rocks are combinations of a great many kinds of minerals, and when you break a piece of rock open, you can see these minerals — such as quartz, calcite, mica, or pyrite.

Here are some minerals that you might find in rocks around your home — as well as some rare and unusual ones.

Quartz

Quartz is probably the commonest of minerals. Quartz may be found in any color of the rainbow or in any combination of colors. It may be as transparent as glass or as opaque as coal. It is one of the hardest of all minerals. It will scratch or cut glass, but it cannot be scratched with a steel knife. Quartz sand is the basic material in glass-making, and crushed quartz is the abrasive we find on sandpaper.

Quartz in granite or on a beach has an irregular shape. But sometimes it is found in the shape of crystals — some long and slender, some short and thick. They are six-sided prisms, with six-sided pyramids on the top.

Mica

Mica is found in granite, shale, and sandstone. It has the peculiar characteristic of being able to split into paper-thin sheets that are transparent, flexible, and fireproof. There are many kinds of mica, but the commonest is known as *muscovite* — so called because large, thick sheets of it were used by the Russians, or Muscovites, to make windowpanes for their homes. Mica is mined commercially in nearly every part of the world and has a great many uses. It is used to make the little "windows" in electric fuses and the larger windows in oven doors — as well as for many other purposes where a heat-proof, transparent material is needed. Crushed, it is the "snow" we put on Christmas trees.

Salt — or Halite

What we call common salt is actually a mineral known as halite — and it is the one solid mineral we cannot do

QUARTZ CRYSTAL   BIOTITE "BLACK MICA"   HALITE   SCORIACEOUS BASALT

without. It is a "must" in everyone's daily diet. In its true form, salt is a perfectly square crystal. Although we get most of our salt from sea water or from deposits on the beds of dried-up lakes, pure rock salt is found in veins under the ground and has been commercially mined for centuries. Where such veins crop out on the surface, wild animals use them as salt licks.

Pyrite

Many miners in the Old West whooped with joy when they broke open rocks and found cubes of this shiny, golden mineral. They thought, of course, that they had struck a lode of gold — but it was actually pyrite, which became known as "fool's gold" because so many people were fooled by it. Large crystals of pyrite are often used to make ornaments and jewelry.

Amber

Amber is not a true mineral, since it is the fossilized residue of the resin of ancient fir trees which long ago toppled into swamps and were covered by mineral-bearing water. But it is an interesting substance to examine. Quite often the bodies of insects that were caught in the resin when it was liquid, thousands of years ago, are still perfectly preserved.

Talc

This curious white mineral is so soft that you can scratch it away with your fingernail, and it feels greasy when you touch it. It is an important industrial product, being used commercially as a lubricant, and is the base for talcum powder.

Calcite

This common mineral is found in a number of forms. It is the main mineral in limestone and in marble. Sometimes you might find a small block of calcite that is as transparent as glass. But the curious thing about it is that when you look through it, you see everything double. This is because the calcite crystals split light rays in two. If you break a calcite crystal with a hammer, each tiny fragment will be a perfect little six-sided shape.

Flexible Sandstone

Here is one of the oddest of all stones. If you take a long, thin slab of it and support it on either end, it will sag in the middle. Then if you turn it over, it will bend the other way. A very thin slab can sometimes be bent until the two ends meet. The reason for the strange behavior of this stone is that it is filled with sheets of mica which overlap each other, allowing the sandstone to flex without breaking and then return to its original shape.

Petrified Wood

Contrary to what most people think, this is not a piece of wood that has turned to stone. What actually happened was this: Millions of years ago, a tree fell into an ancient swamp where the water contained a high proportion of dissolved quartz, which is one of the basic rock-forming minerals. The water soaked into the cells of the wood and, as the wood fibers decayed and rotted away, the quartz hardened into the same pattern as that of the original wood of the tree.

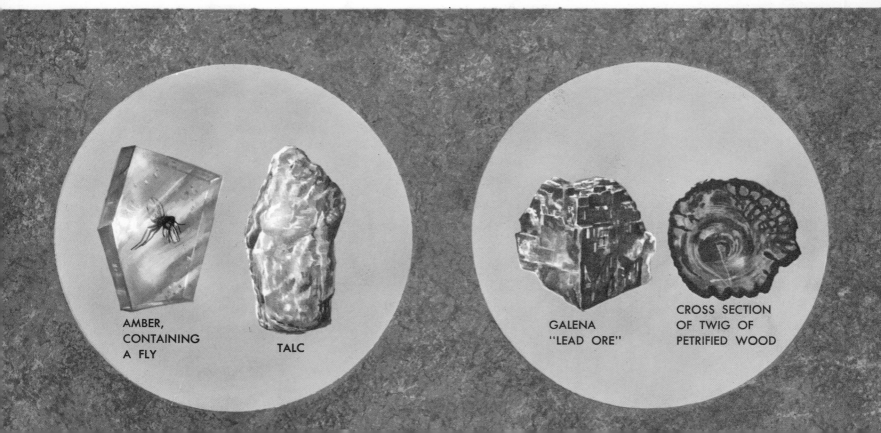

AMBER, CONTAINING A FLY

TALC

GALENA "LEAD ORE"

CROSS SECTION OF TWIG OF PETRIFIED WOOD

The Precious Stones

EVER SINCE the dawn of history, men and women all over the world have treasured rare and beautiful minerals as their most prized possessions. These precious stones became symbols of wealth, rank, social status, and power — as well as religious fetishes and charms.

Foremost among them have been emeralds, rubies, sapphires, opals, turquoise, jade, and diamonds. Diamonds are listed last because, while modern people regard diamonds as the most precious of stones, the ancients valued gems chiefly for their beautiful colors — and since the best diamonds are colorless, they were not particularly popular. The chief use for diamonds in ancient times was for cutting other stones, as a diamond is the hardest of all minerals.

Egyptian craftsmen were extremely adept at carving scarabs and other symbolic objects from gem stones — and hundreds of these priceless relics have been found in the tombs of Egyptian kings. Indians in Mexico and Peru carved religious figures from emeralds, topaz, amethyst, and other precious stones. The British Museum in London exhibits a life-size human skull, perfect down to the slightest detail, carved by an Aztec artist from a single huge crystal of clear quartz. The Chinese made vases, statuettes, and cups from jade and crystal.

Diamonds

In earliest times, almost all diamonds came from India. The jewel center was a town called Golconda, which still gives its name to any place of great riches. Then, not quite a hundred years ago, a small boy playing along the banks of the Orange River in South Africa found a large shiny stone which he took home as a plaything. It proved to be a diamond, and thus began the fabulous diamond rush that established Africa as the world's foremost producer of this most prized of gems.

Diamonds are still found in African rivers, but most of the stones are now taken from mines dug into the blue clay earth in the Union of South Africa. South America also produces a large quantity of diamonds, but most of these are cutting stones, widely used in industry.

The largest diamond ever found, the Cullinan, was discovered by a South African farmer who saw it sticking out of the ground as he walked across a field. It was 3,025¾ carats, about the size of a large man's fist. It has since been cut up to become part of the British crown jewels.

We think of diamonds as clear and colorless, but some of the most famous ones are richly colored. The Hope Diamond is a deep blue, the Dresden Diamond a rich green, the Tiffany Diamond a glittering yellow.

Emeralds

While diamonds are usually considered the most precious of stones, a large flawless emerald is worth considerably more than a diamond of the same size.

In ancient times, the best emeralds were mined in Egypt, and a great many fine stones have been found in Egyptian tombs. Emeralds were also known in Peru and were the royal stones of the Inca kings. When the Spanish conquerors invaded Peru, they stole a fortune in these lovely green jewels. But the fabulous emeralds of Inca legend — many larger than hens' eggs — were hidden from the invaders in secret places known only to the high priests. And there they doubtless still lie today.

Rubies

Most rubies, certainly the finest ones, have always come from Burma. The most valuable of these fiery stones are known as pigeon blood rubies, since from ancient times the standard of perfection has been to compare the color of the stone to that of a drop of blood from a freshly killed pigeon. Perfect rubies are perhaps the rarest of all precious stones.

Sapphires

Sapphires, like rubies, come from the basic mineral, corundum. These gems are found in many hues and colors — but the most valuable are those of a deep cornflower blue which glow with an inner light in the form of a star.

The largest star sapphire, known as the Star of India, weighs 543 carats and is in the collection of the American Museum of Natural History in New York.

Opals

The opal is one of the most beautiful of all precious stones. Unlike most other gems, it is a stone of many colors. The finest ones are flecked with bright glints of red, gold, green, yellow, and purple. Opals have been found in small quantities all over the world since earliest times, but today most of the finest ones come from rich deposits recently discovered in Australia.

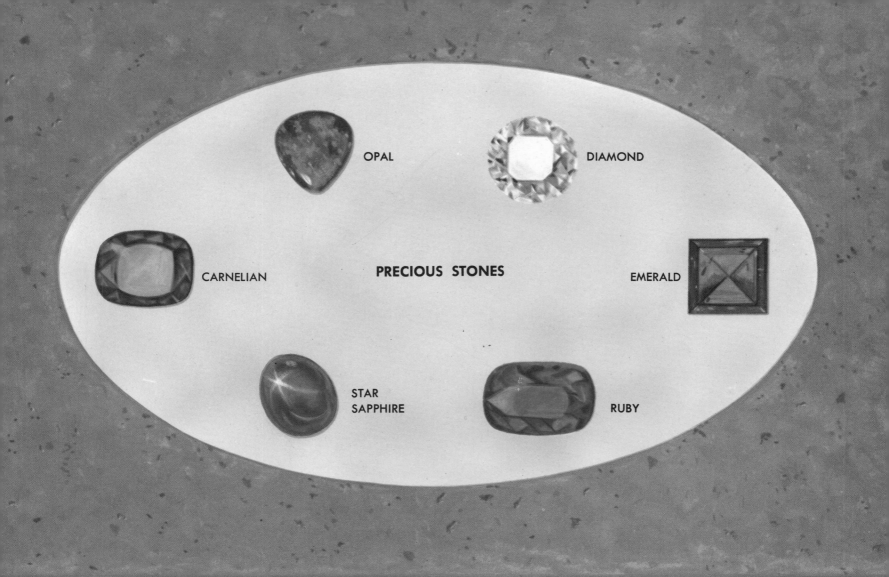

PRECIOUS STONES

OPAL

DIAMOND

CARNELIAN

EMERALD

STAR
SAPPHIRE

RUBY

Legend says that Moses used a diamond to engrave the Ten Commandments on a huge sapphire.

Napoleon finds his lucky carnelian on a battlefield in Egypt.

Legends and Superstitions About Precious Stones

GEM STONES have always been closely linked to religious beliefs and superstitions.

Many people wear their birthstones for good luck: January, garnet; February, amethyst; March, bloodstone; April, diamond; May, emerald; June, pearl or agate; July, ruby; August, moonstone; September, sapphire; October, opal; November, topaz; December, turquoise.

What most birthstone wearers do not know, however, is that this custom originated when each of the twelve tribes of ancient Israel was assigned a particular stone as an identifying token. As time passed, these jewels lost their original meaning and became "birthstones." So if today you wear an amethyst because you were born in February, you might also be saying that you belong to the tribe of Dan.

An early Persian legend says that when God created the world, he made no useless things such as precious stones. But Satan, always eager to cause trouble, created gem stones to make men greedy.

Mohammed is said to have worn a signet ring of carnelian, a stone of flaming red, and so this stone is considered holy by all Moslems to this day. It was also once believed that a carnelian would protect its wearer not only from evil spirits, but also from physical wounds. Napoleon always carried a carnelian, which he had found in Egypt and which he believed shielded him in battle. Apparently it worked, for as far as we know, Napoleon was never wounded in all his many wars.

A polished sphere of quartz crystal — commonly known as a crystal ball — has been used by fortune-tellers for thousands of years as a means of looking into the future. The Romans believed that a cup carved from quartz crystal would not hold poison. So wealthy men always drank from goblets made of this transparent mineral as a safeguard against their enemies.

Diamonds have always been regarded as symbols of purity, love, faith, and joy — and so today diamonds are used in engagement rings. Sometimes diamonds are found in chunks of meteorites that have fallen to the earth. These stones are especially valued as good-luck charms, since they literally came from the heavens.

A dull brown mineral stone called staurolite — better known as "fairy crosses" — is found throughout the southern United States, as well as in other parts of the world. The crystals form a perfect cross, and many people wear them as crucifixes. The story goes that when the fairy

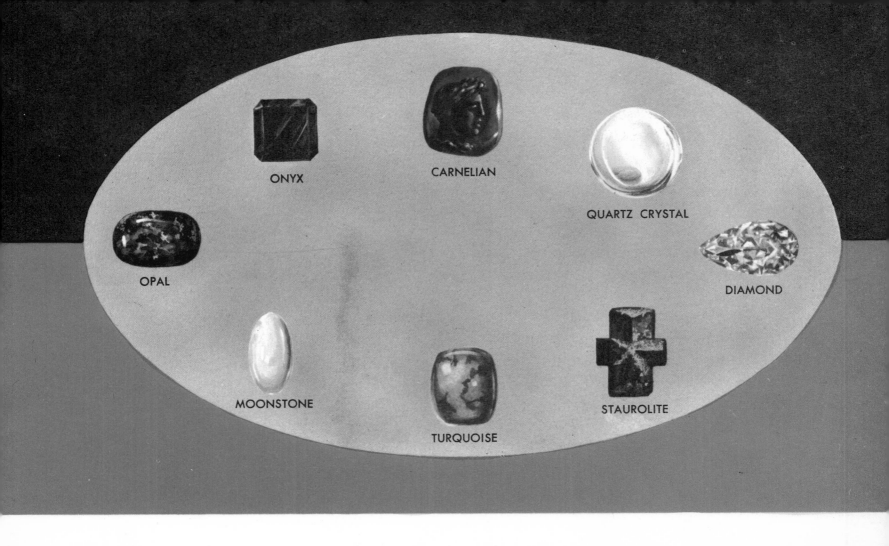

ONYX   CARNELIAN

QUARTZ CRYSTAL

OPAL

DIAMOND

MOONSTONE

STAUROLITE

TURQUOISE

folk learned of the crucifixion of Jesus, they wept tears that fell to the ground in the form of these curious stones.

There was a popular superstition in early Europe that anyone who wore a turquoise could never suffer a broken bone. Instead, the turquoise itself would shatter and thus prevent the accident. The stones were also set into horses' bridles to keep them from stumbling and falling. Today it is quite common for horses' bridles to be decorated with imitation turquoise, although not many people who own them know the origin of the custom.

It is curious how similar superstitions develop in two remotely separated parts of the world. The Aztec Indians of Mexico also believed that turquoise would protect them from physical harm, and warriors used these green and blue stones to decorate their battle shields.

Moonstones are so named because they have a soft, luminous glow akin to moonlight. The Greeks believed that the stones became brighter or dimmer with the phases of the moon, and that when the moon was full the wearer of a moonstone had the power of second sight. A moonstone was also believed to be a powerful good-luck charm, and wearing one was considered a guarantee of success in any undertaking.

Moonstones are found all over the world, mostly on pebbly beaches where they have been washed up by the sea. But nowhere are they so plentiful as on Desolation Island, a dreary place in the south Indian Ocean not far from the Antarctic Circle. Here, in places, the beaches are composed almost entirely of water-polished moonstones.

The opal is one of few precious stones associated with bad luck instead of good. Oddly enough, this superstition does not go back to ancient times but is of fairly recent origin. At the time of the Crimean War in 1853, when opals were very popular jewels in England, a great many dead British soldiers were found on the battlefields wearing rings of this beautiful stone. As a result, other men who wore opal rings took them off before going into battle. And this superstition has persisted to a great extent to this day.

The ancient Chinese believed that the onyx held a demon imprisoned inside it, and that he came out at night to bring bad luck to anyone who was near. For this reason the onyx, which we usually see in the form of a cameo, was never used as jewelry in China.

In India the owner of a fiery red ruby was believed to be safe at all times, for if some danger were near, the stone would warn its wearer by suddenly becoming dark.

Common Gem Stones

ALONG with the occasional diamond or sapphire that some lucky finder picks up in a field or a stream bed, nearly a hundred different kinds of handsome semi-precious gem stones can be found all over the United States by people who know where to look for them — and who recognize them when they see them.

In fact, next to stamp collecting, stone collecting is America's most popular hobby. Many people who started the habit of picking up pretty pebbles when they were children, carry on this fascinating hobby all their lives.

Any boy or girl who keeps his eyes open is likely to find many interesting gem stones within walking distance of his front door. A stream bed is the easiest place to find them, for the water has already dug them out of the ground and given them a little polish. Other likely places are gravel pits, excavations, or rock quarries where the face of the rock strata has been cut into.

The seashore, of course, is a great treasure trove for gem hunters. The incoming waves keep constantly replenishing the supply, and many stones of real value have been found on beaches that have been picked over for years.

Many people become so interested in gem collecting that they equip themselves with cutting and grinding tools and polish the finer stones they find into jewelry pieces that rival any to be found in a jewelry store.

Here are some of the most popular gem stones found in the United States.

AQUAMARINE. This lovely stone — usually pale bluish-green or sea-green — is found in the form of clear transparent crystals, most often embedded in surrounding rock. It is a close relative of the emerald, the chief difference being in the deep, rich, green color that gives the emerald its distinction, its rarity, and its value.

The largest gem of any kind ever found was a flawless aquamarine crystal, about the size of a small barrel, which weighed 220 pounds. The Brazilian Indian who discovered it could see through it perfectly from end to end. Realizing that such a wonderfully clear stone must be of unusual value, he took it out of the jungle in his canoe — a very difficult job, as you can imagine. It was finally cut up into 200,000 carats of superb gem stones.

CLEAR QUARTZ. Sometimes one is lucky enough to find a clear quartz crystal with a little hollow cavity inside containing a drop or two of water. This water somehow became imprisoned inside the stone when the crystal was formed, and of course since it cannot evaporate, it will remain there forever.

AGATE. This is a form of quartz which usually has concentric layers of several different colors. When it is cut and polished, agate makes rings and jewelry of gleaming beauty.

AMETHYST. These delicate purple crystals are in great demand for ladies' rings and other jewelry. They are found almost everywhere in the United States. Usually they are in clusters of dozens, or hundreds, of small crystal forms.

TOURMALINE. This interesting stone is usually found embedded in quartz rock. Several colors, ranging from green to pink to blue, may be found in the same crystal, such as the unusually large one pictured here.

SUN STONE (or GOLDSTONE). Tiny specks of colored mica embedded in clear quartz crystal give this unusual stone the appearance of having flashing sparks of fire burning deep down inside it.

TOPAZ. Most people think of a topaz as yellow, and, indeed, the word has become a synonym for anything of a yellow hue. But a topaz may also be white, brown, or blue.

GARNET. Ordinary garnets are abundant all over America, in the hills of New England and the South as well as on the deserts of the West. Most are of a brownish color, but the most prized stones are a deep clear red or sometimes an emerald green.

CHALCEDONY. The smooth, round, semi-transparent pebbles that you often find on beaches or along the banks of streams are usually chalcedony, which is a kind of quartz. A colored variety of this stone, usually red but sometimes yellow or green, is known as *jasper*.

OBSIDIAN. This is a volcanic glass. The Indians used it for arrowheads and knives. When polished, it takes on an extremely high luster. It may be black, brown, red, gray, or green — and is semitransparent.

Some other common gem stones and their colors are BERYL (green or bluish green); RHODONITE (pink, brownish or yellow); PLASMA (green); BLOODSTONE (green and dotted with red spots, also called HELIOTROPE); and MARCASITE (greenish white).

The seashore is the best place to look for interesting stones.

CHALCEDONY

OBSIDIAN

AQUAMARINE

CLEAR QUARTZ

GARNET

COMMON GEM STONES

AGATE

TOPAZ

GOLDSTONE

TOURMALINE

AMETHYST

Metals That Make Our Modern World

Iron and Steel

OF ALL the minerals we use in our modern world, the most important is iron.

Although iron was one of the four most abundant elements from which our earth was made — and although geologists believe that the earth's central core is almost pure iron — iron in its pure state practically never appears on the surface where man can get at it. Instead, iron is mixed with other minerals in the form of *ore,* and the ore itself is embedded in the rock of the crust. Extracting it is a long and difficult process.

The most important deposit of iron ore in the United States is around Lake Superior. Here some of the ore lies near the surface, and it is scooped out of great open pits by steam shovels.

The ore is then shipped in cargo vessels through the Great Lakes to the mills of Ohio and Pennsylvania, where it is converted into steel. This is how it is done.

The crushed ore is put into a huge blast furnace, along with coke and limestone. The burning coke generates extreme heat which melts the iron from the worthless parts of the ore. In the process the iron also picks up

carbon from the coke. As this melting goes on, the limestone fuses with the impurities in the ore, floats them to the top of the liquid metal, and carries them away in the form of slag.

The pure iron thus extracted from the ore in which it was imprisoned is further refined and converted into steel, which is many times stronger and harder than the original iron, but pliable enough to be molded into such shapes as automobile bodies and watch springs.

Copper

Next to iron, copper is our most useful metal. It is essential to the manufacture of electrical equipment, although it has many other uses as well. In alloy, or mixed, with zinc, it becomes brass; and when tin is added to the alloy, it is bronze.

Copper is found both in veins in its pure state and mixed with other minerals in ore. The most important deposits of copper in the United States are in Montana.

Furnaces refining iron ore in a modern steel mill

Aluminum

There is even more aluminum than iron in the great mass of minerals that make up the earth's crust. But most of it is imprisoned in silicate rock, and there is no practical method by which it can be extracted.

However, under certain conditions, these rocks have weathered and broken down into a claylike mineral called *bauxite*. And it is from this bauxite that we get all of the aluminum we use in industry.

Aluminum is a very light, very strong metal, and it is used where lightness is as important as strength.

Chromium

Stainless steel — which is used for automobile accessories, plumbing fixtures, and other products that require extreme hardness plus resistance to rust — is an alloy of steel and chromium. Small deposits of chromium are found in the United States, but we import most of what we use from Africa and Asia. The chief source of chromium is the mineral *chromite*.

Other Metals

There are a great many other important metals.

ZINC is chiefly used as a coating for iron and steel to protect them from rust, and as an alloy with copper in brass and bronze.

TIN is most generally used to put a protective coating over steel so that the food in "tin" cans will not spoil.

LEAD was used in ancient Rome to make water pipes, and our word "plumbing" comes from the Latin word for lead, *plumbum*. Lead has many uses today, principally in protective shields for radioactive materials and as the anti-knock ingredient in gasoline.

NICKEL, an extremely rugged metal, is employed in alloys with steel and copper. Our five-cent coin, the nickel, is 25 per cent nickel and 75 per cent copper.

MERCURY, sometimes called quicksilver, is the most unusual metal of them all. Its melting point is far below that of ice, so that we never see it in solid form except in a laboratory. Mercury is extremely sensitive to changes in pressure and temperature, and its chief use is in making thermometers and other scientific instruments.

Precious Metals

Gold

IT IS a strange thing that the metal we generally consider to be the most precious is, in fact, the most useless. Wars have been fought, nations have been conquered, millions of people have been murdered or enslaved — all for the sake of gold. Yet aside from the fact that it makes pretty jewelry, gold is virtually good for nothing, being much too soft and structurally too weak for practical industrial purposes.

Even in what are called "solid gold" rings and jewelry, gold must be alloyed with harder metals in order for it to stand up under everyday wear. This leads to the many varieties of gold which we see in jewelry today. *White gold* is an alloy of gold and platinum. *Green gold* is gold and silver. *Red gold* is gold and copper.

Gold serves as the standard of the world's money system, yet you never see a gold coin because it is against the law to have one in your possession. Except for the small amount used in jewelry making, all the gold mined in the United States and much of that mined in foreign countries is shaped into bricks and buried again underneath the ground at Fort Knox, Kentucky, in order to protect the value of our money.

And yet, gold has probably been the greatest single incentive in the development of modern civilization. America was discovered and our great western states were settled because of man's endless search for gold. It was the lure of gold that led to the colonization of Alaska, Australia, and Central Africa.

Gold is found in veins in rocks that are rich in quartz. When these rocks weather and break down, the gold mixes with the resulting gravel and mud in the form of small grains or sometimes larger nuggets. This mixture of gold dust, earth, and gravel is known to miners as "pay dirt."

Gold exists in small quantities everywhere. If you knew how to do it — and if you worked long and patiently enough — you could probably pan a small amount of gold out of any creek. But only in a few places on earth are gold deposits rich enough to make it practical for miners to work them.

The richest gold deposits in the United States are in California. When gold was first discovered there, in 1848, millions of dollars worth of the gleaming metal was washed from the sand and rocks of stream beds. There are still placer miners — mostly old-timers — who make their living by panning gold from the beds of the Feather and American rivers in California, the very streams in which gold was first discovered.

Most gold, however, is taken from underground mines. The gold-bearing ore is crushed, and the gold is separated by a chemical process. Most of the world's gold today comes from mines in South Africa.

Silver

Like gold, silver is frequently found in its pure form, as well as combined in ore with other minerals. Also like gold, it is a favorite metal for making jewelry. Since it is more plentiful than gold, silver is not as expensive and so is used for the manufacture of fine tableware. Yet it is still too costly for wide industrial use. Money is coined from silver in every country of the world.

Neither air nor water can rust or corrode silver. It tarnishes easily because certain gases in the air react to it to produce a thin film of *silver sulfide*. But this is easily removed without harm to the metal.

Silver is the best known conductor of heat and electricity. For this reason it is used in the finest electrical equipment where cost is not a factor. Silver is also used with other minerals and chemicals, such as chlorine, bromine, and iodine, to make photographic film sensitive to light.

Platinum

One of the rarest metals in the world, platinum was first discovered in South America about the middle of the eighteenth century. Its real value was not suspected in the early days and, since it had many of the properties of gold, it was minted into counterfeit coins which were then covered by a thin gold film. Many people later made fortunes by collecting these counterfeit coins, which were originally considered worthless, but which were actually worth more than if they had been solid gold in the first place.

Platinum is the most ductile of all metals. One ounce of it, a chunk not much larger than a pea, can be drawn out into a length of wire so fine that it would stretch from New York to Omaha. In addition to its use in the manufacture of fine and expensive jewelry, platinum is also used for making laboratory instruments.

Uranium

Uranium is the "miracle metal" of the twentieth century. Not much more than twenty years ago, its chief use was for coloring pottery and glassware and giving a shiny luster to false teeth.

Then almost overnight came the fantastic age of atomic energy and the dramatic discovery that uranium was the most important source of this great power. Suddenly uranium became the world's most sought-after metal.

Uranium is the energy-source of the atomic bomb — and it is this same explosive power that runs an atomic power plant for peacetime use. But the uranium in an atomic reactor — instead of exploding all at once in a blinding flash — gives off its energy in a carefully controlled trickle. Thus, using a piece of uranium no larger than a light bulb as fuel, a submarine like the *Nautilus* can cruise at top speed for more than 100,000 miles.

Some other ores in which uranium is found are Uranite, Pitchblende (a form of Uranite), Carnotite, Davidite, Torbernite, Samarskite and Gummite.

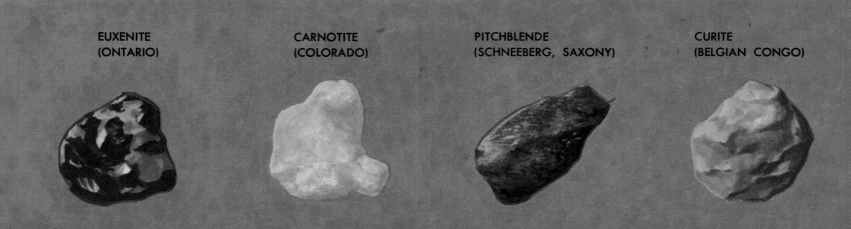

EUXENITE
(ONTARIO)

CARNOTITE
(COLORADO)

PITCHBLENDE
(SCHNEEBERG, SAXONY)

CURITE
(BELGIAN CONGO)

Oil – Our Most Important Fuel

VIRTUALLY all of the world's oil comes out of sedimentary rocks such as sandstone and limestone. Most of these rocks were laid down in ancient seas, although some oil-producing rocks mark the locations of extinct swamps and lakes. The petroleum was formed from the remains of living things, both plant and animal. Our oldest sedimentary rocks have little or no petroleum in them — simply because there just wasn't enough organic matter to produce oil.

Recently scientists have shown that petroleum hydrocarbons are forming in the muds of modern lakes, swamps and seas. However, there is not enough of this petroleum in the process of formation to be economically valuable. It seems to take millions of years to produce an oil field.

Conditions that led to the formation of petroleum in pre-historic times were not too different from those in comparable places today. There were various types of fish in the ocean, shelled animals and seaweeds waving in ancient currents. Plants and animals were different from modern ones, but probably existing in similar ways. As these plants and animals died, their remains settled to the sea floor, even as they do today, to be buried by sand and mud that drifted out from the land.

As time went on, more and more organic sediments formed and were buried deep beneath newer layers of sedimentary deposits. These eventually solidified into sedimentary rocks, the sea retreated to other places, and the ancient sea bottom became dry land.

While all this was going on, a curious thing happened. Pressures from inside the earth — and other forces that we still do not know too much about — brought about a chemical change in the masses of animal and vegetable matter that had sunk into the original deposit many millions of years before. It became an underground reservoir of petroleum.

Sometimes these underground deposits came close enough to the surface so that the oil seeped up and formed black sticky puddles. In places, the earth's internal pressures forced it up through fissures in the rock so that it squirted out in a fountain. When Marco Polo returned from his famous journey to Asia, in 1295, he told of such natural geysers of oil.

Earlier the Greeks and Romans had soaked wads of cotton in this crude oil — which they called pitch — ignited them, and hurled the fiery balls from catapults against enemy ships and cities.

The American Indians used oil from natural seepages as medicine, and the early settlers followed their example. Traveling peddlers and medicine-show doctors bottled it and sold it throughout the countryside as "Indian Oil" or "Seneca Oil." People rubbed it on their bodies to cure rheumatism and took it internally as medicine.

Then, not much more than one hundred years ago, it was discovered that petroleum could be refined into kerosene, and that this made a much better fuel for lamps than anything then in use. But since the only source of supply was from natural seepages, petroleum was very scarce and expensive.

It had been noticed that often the water in wells was spoiled by streaks of oil mixed with it. This occurred quite frequently in the vicinity of Titusville, a small town in western Pennsylvania. Finally, a group of businessmen formed a company to drill for the oil itself.

They employed Colonel Edwin L. Drake to take charge of the drilling, and in 1859 the first oil well in America was sunk. Colonel Drake and his helpers laboriously began drilling through layers of solid rock. It was hard work, and the townspeople came out in the evenings to scoff and jeer. They called the well "Drake's Folly."

But, without knowing it, Colonel Drake had picked the best of all possible places for his attempt. The area around Titusville was underlaid with vast deposits of petroleum, from which we still get some of our best grades of lubricating oil. And so, after months of back-breaking toil, Drake's drills finally broke through into an oil reservoir, and the world's first oil well began producing in quantity.

As the diagram on the right shows, oil deposits are usually trapped under the ground between layers of folded rock. The petroleum floats on a reservoir of water, with a pocket of natural gas on top. Sometimes the pressure is so great that when the drill penetrates the rock, the oil and gas shoot out in a tremendous gusher.

It has been estimated that the earth's total reserve of petroleum is about 610 billion barrels, and that we have already used up about one tenth of it. The present world consumption is some 18 million barrels a day, and this is increasing all the time.

Some day — and at the rate industry is speeding up, it may not be too far in the future — all of the earth's oil deposits will be gone. Then the world will have to look elsewhere for its fuel supply. Scientists believe that the ultimate answer may lie in atomic energy.

Above, the first stage in the formation of oil on an ocean floor.

Below, a typical oil deposit trapped between layers of rock.

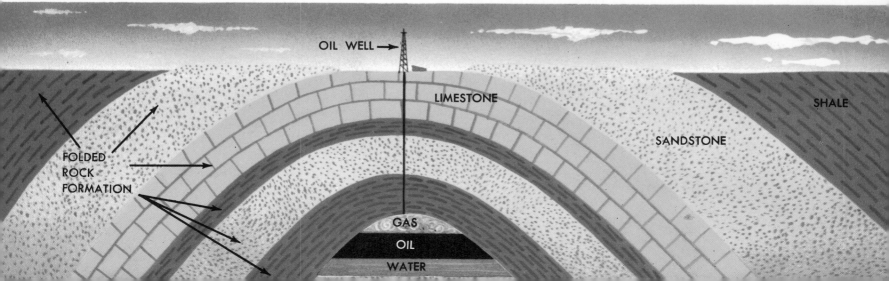

OIL WELL →

LIMESTONE

SHALE

SANDSTONE

FOLDED
ROCK
FORMATION

GAS

OIL

WATER

Coal

COAL, like petroleum — was formed from organic matter. But coal is completely the product of plants. Vast masses of vegetable matter — trees, herbs, vines, ferns and shrubs — fell into primeval swamps about 200 to 250 million years ago and were covered by mud and silt which turned into stone.

But during this long period, the tree ferns and mosses — instead of changing into liquid oil — were subjected to forces which transformed them into the hard, black, brittle rock that we call coal.

Sometimes when a piece of coal is broken open, the fossil imprint of a fern leaf can be clearly seen, still as perfectly shaped as when it grew upon the ancient tree.

Coal lies under the ground in long, thick seams, sandwiched between layers of sandstone or shale.

When the coal lies in rock folds in hilly country, miners tunnel directly into the seam from the side of a hill. This is called a *drift mine*.

When the coal lies deep underground, shafts are sunk straight down to the seam, and the miners tunnel outward from the shaft through the seam itself. This is a *shaft mine*.

Sometimes the coal lies so close to the surface that it can be dug out with steam shovels, in much the same way that iron ore is mined. This is called *strip mining*.

Next to wood, coal is the oldest of fuels. The Chinese mined it as long ago as 1000 B.C. and used it to smelt iron and copper. Coal fires are mentioned in the Old Testament. We know that, at about the time of Christ, coal was used by the Romans during their occupation of England, for coal and coal ashes have been found in ancient Roman ruins.

American Indians used the "rock that burns" long before the first voyage of Columbus. And medieval blacksmiths used coal for heating the iron with which they worked.

Coal powered the industrial revolution in England. When James Watt's invention of the steam engine, in 1765, made large industrial machines possible, coal was the perfect fuel to keep the machines running. For the first time, coal mining became a major industry and an important factor in the world's economy.

The first coal mine in America, located in Virginia and opened in 1745, provided fuel for making weapons for the Revolutionary armies. But the use of coal was limited because there was no way to transport it in quantity. This problem was solved by the development of railroads, and by the time of the War Between the States, coal was the power behind America's rapidly growing industry.

As it has been from the beginning, coal is still a vital factor in our industrial economy. It fuels the power plants that generate three-quarters of all our electrical energy. Its chemical by-products provide the essential materials for one third of our chemical industry. In the United States alone, 100 million tons each year are processed into *coke*.

We have seen that coke is an essential ingredient in the manufacture of steel. This is how it is made.

Coal is fed into a large enclosed oven, and the opening is sealed. Then gas is pumped in and ignited. Although the temperature rises to more than 2,000 degrees, lack of oxygen inside the oven keeps the coal from burning. Instead, the oils and gases in the coal are distilled and piped from the oven as by-products to be converted into tars, ammonias, acids, and other chemical raw materials.

After about nineteen hours, the finished coke is taken from the oven and sprinkled with water to keep it from bursting into flame upon contact with the air. At this point it is a gray substance, about 90 per cent carbon, and capable of creating the intense, concentrated heat required for the smelting of iron ore.

Coal deposits are found all over the world, although about 95 per cent of them are concentrated in the Northern Hemisphere, and coal reserves in tropical countries are very thin indeed. The United States has nearly half of the world's coal, with Russia second and China third.

In America alone, we burn up 400 million tons of coal each year, and the rest of the world uses about the same amount. But scientists tell us that this is only a tiny fraction of the total reserves beneath the earth's surface. It is estimated that the staggering total of some seven trillion tons is still untouched — enough to last at the present rate of consumption for the next 2,000 years.

However, some geologists consider this estimate to be low. We know, for example, that large coal deposits lie under the icecap of the Antarctic continent, but at present there is no way of determining how extensive they may be.

In spite of the tremendous amount of coal we consume yearly, its use as a fuel is declining compared to that of oil. But many scientists believe that the most important function of coal in the future will be not as a fuel, but as an almost endless source of chemical raw materials.

Plant material accumulated in ancient swamp forests was eventually buried. Then, after millions of years, nature slowly transformed this material into what we call coal.

The Earth's Magic Carpet

THE SOIL is a living carpet that covers and brightens the bare rock of the earth's floor.

Unlike most carpets, it is not of uniform thickness. It is deepest in tropical countries, where luxuriant vegetation grows all year round and keeps constantly replenishing it. It becomes thinner as one goes north or south toward the poles. In the jungles of Africa and South America, the carpet of soil may be twenty to forty feet deep. In northern countries, where recurring glaciers have bulldozed it away, there is sometimes only an inch or two of soil laid over the crustal rock.

The soil nourishes all life on land. Without it, no grass or grain or vegetables could grow to furnish food for animals or men. And when the life cycle of the plants is completed, they go back into the soil to nourish it in turn.

Soil is a combination of decaying rock and decaying vegetable matter. The hot summer sun heats bare rock and expands and cracks it. The ice and snow of winter contracts 'and splits it. Rain washes tiny grains of the weathered rock into small depressions in the land. There the rock particles mingle with dead leaves and decaying plants, and the two form the carpet of soil that covers the earth's surface.

You can prove this to yourself by dropping a handful of soil from your garden into a glass of water. Stir it well, and then let it settle. Some particles will float to the top. The rest will settle to the bottom. If you examine the floating particles, you will see that they are tiny bits and pieces of leaves and roots and other vegetable matter. The heavier particles that sink are sand and bits of gravel — actually, the small remnants of weathered and broken rocks.

We have seen that all water is on a never-ending journey to the sea. The same is true of soil, and it is water that carries it on its way. As the rocks of mountains are weathered and eventually worn down to become soil, the rivers move them toward the ocean in the form of mud and silt.

When a stream floods and overflows its banks, the muddy waters spread the soil out in a thin layer over new land. Then rains ultimately wash it back into the rivers, and it continues on toward the sea.

But for every ounce of soil that is washed away, another takes its place. And so the only way in which we are aware that the soil is moving is when we look at the muddy water rushing along a riverbed.

How the Soil Was Created

DURING most of the earth's lifetime of four to five billion years, it had no soil. There was nothing on the face of the land but barren rock. As the rocks were weathered by the sun, wind, and rain, they were washed down to the sea and new rock formations rose up to take their place.

Then, scientists believe, tiny lichenlike plants from the sea water began to grow on rocks at the ocean's edge. Their tiny roots penetrated the rocks' surfaces and caused bits of them to scale off. As the lichens died and decayed, they mingled with the rock dust and gradually began to turn into soil. This primitive soil took minerals from the rocks and the air and the water, and at last the long, slow process of building up a permanent soil carpet began.

More plants grew, and in turn became part of the soil when they withered and died. In this way the carpet of soil began creeping inland from the shores of the sea until, after millions of years, it covered the whole earth.

If you could see a typical cross section of the soil, you would observe that it is divided into three layers.

The bottom, or "C," layer is solid bedrock, with its upper edges slowly decomposing and flaking off.

The middle, or "B," layer is hard-packed and contains rock fragments and pebbles mixed with clay and heavy earth. Minerals seep down into it from the surface and up from the ground water that lies underneath. Only the roots of trees and larger plants penetrate the "B" layer.

The top, or "A," layer is the part of the soil in which we plant things. It is soft and crumbly and is composed sometimes almost entirely of decayed vegetable matter. This is the layer in which most of the underground life goes on.

In addition to the minerals that make things grow and the plant roots that reach down into it for food, the earth's magic carpet is literally teeming with animal life. Every square foot of the soil contains billions of tiny bacteria and microbes so small that they cannot be seen without a microscope.

When the body of an animal or the trunk of a fallen tree is lying on the ground or is covered by the soil, these bacteria attack it at once and in time consume it completely. Even in the coldest arctic regions, this activity goes on unchecked. Eskimos bury sealskins so that the bacteria will remove the hairs from the leather.

For, a few feet under the surface, the soil knows no seasons. The earth's magic carpet is as warm in Alaska as it is in Zanzibar.

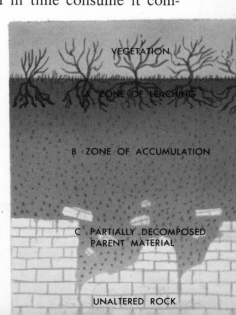

VEGETATION

A ZONE OF LEACHING

B ZONE OF ACCUMULATION

C PARTIALLY DECOMPOSED PARENT MATERIAL

UNALTERED ROCK

Creatures of the Soil

THE EARTHWORM is Nature's tiller of the soil. Long before man invented the first primitive plow, these curious creatures were keeping the carpet of soil loose and porous by the simple process of eating their way through it. The earthworm gets its nourishment from the organic matter in the soil, and in turn fertilizes the soil with minerals from its body.

Earthworms are found all over the world's temperate zones and are usually thickest in the leafmold loam of hardwood forests. In certain places, it has been estimated that there are more than a million worms under each acre. You rarely find them in pine forests because they cannot live in the acid soil created by fallen pine needles.

You have probably noticed that after a heavy rain earthworms may be seen squirming about on the surface of the ground. This is because the rain water has streamed down into their burrows and flooded them out — a good example of how the earthworm's constant digging allows air and water to penetrate into the ground and keep the soil rich and fruitful.

Earthworms vary in size from the common night crawlers, which people use for bait when they go fishing, to the giant worms of Australia which are sometimes ten or twelve feet long and as big around as a broomstick.

The SCARAB BEETLE is one of the hardest workers of all the insects that live in the soil. It is also one of the worst thieves.

This beetle scours dirt and filth from the surface of the ground and laboriously rolls it into a ball of food, usually several times larger than its body. Then, backing up and pushing the ball, the scarab rolls it to a place where the earth is soft and easy to dig. Moving the ball is a long hard job, and often it takes hours for the beetle to roll it to its place. But once it succeeds in getting it there, it begins to scoop out a tunnel in the ground.

Quite often, while the scarab bettle is digging its hole, another beetle comes along and steals the ball. Then the victim has to go to the trouble of collecting another one — unless it, in turn, can steal one from a neighbor. But if it still has the ball when its digging job is finished, it rolls the ball to the hole, drops it in, and goes in after it.

Then the scarab covers the entrance to the hole with leaves and small sticks and settles down to enjoy its hard-earned meal. It eats until it has consumed the entire ball and then it goes to the surface again and begins to collect another one.

The CICADA is sometimes known as the "seventeen-year locust." It spends the first seventeen years of its life buried in the soil, and then it emerges for a brief three or four weeks as a winged insect.

The mother cicada lays her eggs on the leaves of trees during her short life in the sunlight. When they hatch out, the young grubs tumble to the ground and immediately dig themselves in. There the tiny wormlike crea-

EARTHWORM

SCARAB BEETLE

CICADA (EMERGING)

tures remain for seventeen years, drinking the sap of roots to get their nourishment. After the seventeen years have passed, they respond to some mysterious urge and dig a tunnel to the surface.

However, they do not leave the tunnel at once. Instead, they lie at its bottom, often for weeks, waiting for the signal to come forth. Just what the signal is, no one knows. But all the cicadas receive it at the same time. They then creep up to the surface in one vast migration.

On the first day they shed their shell-like skins and change into flying insects with long bodies and delicate wings. They take off in great swarms and eat all the vegetation in sight. During this stage, they mate, lay their eggs, and at last complete their fantastic life cycle.

At the end of three or four weeks they are all dead. But the eggs they have laid on the tree leaves will soon be hatched. And another generation of cicadas will again be burrowing into the ground to begin their long sleep.

WASPS dig a large round cellar about two feet deep under the ground, usually the size of a large pumpkin. Inside this hole they build their nest, suspending it from root ends in much the same way that a hornet's nest is suspended from the limbs of a tree.

The nest itself is constructed from a thin paper-like material which the wasp makes by chewing up bits of wood. The nest hangs free in the underground cellar, with a space left between the walls of the nest and the sides of the cellar so that the wasp workers can come and go in their never-ending task of enlarging the nest as the colony grows.

Inside the nest, the wasps build combs of the same wood pulp material, and it is here that they store the honey that they gather each day from flowers. In addition to the honey that they store away, they vary their diet with flies, grubs, and other insects which they sting to death and draw down into their underground city.

TRAP-DOOR SPIDERS are usually found on our western deserts. They build curious nests in the soft sand which are both a home for themselves and an ingenious trap for any unwary insect that might have the misfortune to stroll by.

The spider digs a long, thin burrow down into the earth, which it lines with silk. At the top it constructs a door, made of layers of silk and wet sand. The door is so heavy that it falls shut when the spider releases it, and on the underside the spider makes a handle so that it can hold the door shut at will.

Each evening the spider props open its door and waits for a victim to happen along. When some unfortunate insect wanders within range, the spider nabs it, pulls it down into its nest, lets the door fall shut, and then proceeds to eat its dinner at leisure.

The trap-door spider has one deadly enemy — the *pepsis wasp*. And for some strange reason it makes no attempt to defend itself when the pepsis attacks, even though it is many times larger than its foe. When a pepsis approaches a trap-door spider, the spider seems to be paralyzed with fear. It doesn't try to run away or fight back. Instead, it seems to accept its fate and allows itself to be killed without offering any resistance.

WASPS
(NEST SHOWN CUT AWAY)

TRAP-DOOR SPIDER

PEPSIS WASP
(STINGING TRAP-DOOR SPIDER)

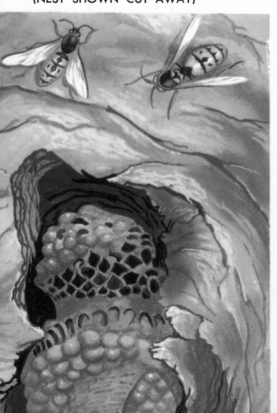

The Wonderful World of Ants

HAVE YOU ever turned over a flat rock in a field and seen dozens of ants scurrying along the runways that furrow the ground?

This is the roof of an underground ant city, which may extend as much as ten or twenty feet into the soft soil, and contain as many floors and rooms as the Empire State Building. The rooms are connected by long halls, inclined ramps go from one floor to the next, and streets provide a means of getting from one place to another.

In their wonderful world underneath the ground, the ants live an amazing life. Some raise crops for food. Others tend herds of "milk cows." One ant city may make war on another, and then the victors bring back captured slaves to serve them. There are queen ants, soldier ants, policeman ants, engineering ants, and builder ants.

Slave-owning Ants

Ants have a reputation as industrious workers, and most of them are. But there are some warlike tribes that don't like to work. They capture ants from other tribes, enslave them, and make the captives do all their work.

One of the commonest of these slave-holding ants is the *Sanguin*. It is a big, strong, vicious, fighting ant and its bite can even make a human go "yip!"

Two or three times a year, the Sanguin army goes on a slaving raid. They usually pick on small, black, peaceful, hard-working ants known as the *Fuscas*. The Sanguins first send out a scouting part to locate a Fusca city. Then the army advances in battle order and attacks.

The Fuscas try to defend their city, but they are no match for the Sanguins. The raiders quickly kill the guards and enter the city. First they slaughter all the adult Fuscas. Then they take the Fusca eggs and carry them back to the Sanguin city. They also carry along the bodies of the dead Fuscas for food.

When the Fusca eggs hatch out, the little black ants don't know that they have been made prisoners. They only know that they are supposed to wait on the Sanguins, feed them, keep them clean, and do all the work. Since they have never known any other life, they happily accept their roles as slaves.

Sometimes the Sanguins decide that the Fusca city that they have just looted is better than their own. In this case they desert their old city, and the whole Sanguin tribe moves into the one they have captured.

Ant Farmers

As far as we know, the ant is the only creature besides man that plants, cultivates, and harvests its own food. The most common of these farmer ants is the *Atta,* or parasol ant, found in the southern United States and Central and South America. The crop that is grown on their underground farms is mushrooms.

The Attas climb trees and cut round pieces of leaves, each about the size of a quarter. These they carry back to their city, holding the leaf sections over their heads like parasols. Where Attas are especially numerous they become great pests, for they can destroy an entire grove of fruit trees by cutting off all the leaves.

After the porters bring the leaves home, workers chew them into a fine compost on which a special kind of very tiny mushroom sprouts. The ants tend their mushroom beds as carefully as a farmer tends his fields. They weed them constantly to keep them clear of foreign fungus growth, and transplant them as the colony grows.

When the Attas move to a new city, they are careful to take along "seeds" with which to start new crops.

Harvester Ants

Unlike the parasol ants, harvesters do not grow their own food. Instead, they gather wild seeds which they store in underground granaries.

The harvesters cut wide roads through the grass, which extend out from the roof of the city like spokes from the hub of a wheel. Every morning the tribe sets off down these roads to the places they have selected for their seed picking. Each ant gathers one seed, carries it back to the city, and returns to get another one. All day long a double procession of ants files along the roads — one line carrying seeds, the other returning for another load.

When the seeds are delivered at the city, special workers husk them and spread them out to dry. Then they carry them to the storerooms below.

Often the ants work in teams to save time. One ant will climb to the top of a tall stem, pick off all the seeds, and drop them to others on the ground below. If they find seeds that are too heavy for a single ant to carry, several ants will get together and carry one seed between them, in much the same way that three or four men carry a piano or other heavy object.

Sanguin ant carrying egg of Fusca ant. When hatched, the Fusca becomes a slave of the Sanguins.

Above, Atta ants carrying pieces of leaves to their city.

Harvester ant, below, carrying a seed along the ant road, back to the nest.

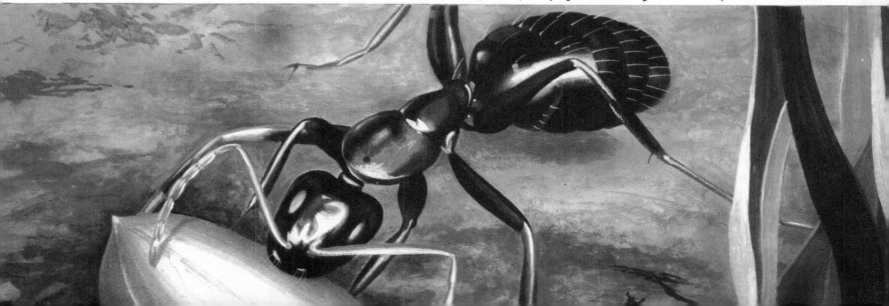

Rancher ant, with herd of cows

Ant Ranchers

If you look closely at the leaves of a tree in summer, you may see several hundred tiny white insects grazing contentedly on the green pasturage. With them, protecting them and keeping them from straying, will be about a dozen ants.

The little white insects are *aphids,* and they are the ants' "milk cows."

Just as a cow gives milk, an aphid gives a sweet, clear fluid called *honeydew* which the ants like very much to drink. For this reason the ants herd the aphids and look after them in the same way that a dairy farmer tends his herd of cows.

Every fall the ants raid aphid nests and carry off the eggs. They place them in snug barns in the ant city and watch over them until the little aphids hatch out in the spring. When warm weather comes, they put their herds out to pasture on the vast acres of fresh leaves.

The natural enemies of the aphids are ladybugs and wasps. Alone, they are helpless against these foes. But the ant cowboys are fierce fighters, and the aphid "cows" have no need to worry while the ant herders are there to protect them.

A single aphid gives enough honeydew each day to feed several ants, and ant "milkmaids" hurry back and forth all day long from the pasture to the city.

At the approach of winter, the aphids die. But the busy ants have stored away a supply of "milk" to last them until spring, and they have also brought in a new batch of aphid eggs which will become next year's herd of cows.

The Amazing Termite

Sometimes called "white ants," termites live the most complex and highly organized life of any of Nature's underground creatures.

Termites are blind. Yet in spite of this handicap, they are highly skilled engineers and builders. On the African plains they construct huge mud buildings so solid in substance that they are impervious to wind, rain, or the picks and shovels of man. A large tree can fall on such a termite hill without doing it any damage.

These termite cities are miracles of engineering. There are large warehouses for food storage, a huge palace for the king and queen, barracks for the soldiers and police, and living quarters for the city's millions of workers. Literally miles of hard mud streets crisscross the termite

QUEEN

TUNNELS TO OTHER CHAMBERS

KING

TERMITES

The king and queen in the "throne room" of a termite city.

city. They wind up the sides of open places like switchbacks on our roads in the Rocky Mountains. And at some points large open places are crossed by superbly engineered suspension bridges, many of which are relatively much longer than the Golden Gate and George Washington bridges. All of the streets and bridges, as well as the termites' road systems outside their city, are built for two-way traffic — and, amazingly enough, termite traffic keeps to the right, just as we do in our automobiles.

Termites live on a natural diet of dead wood. This was fine as long as they had the forests to themselves — and termites are one of the oldest existing species of animal life on earth — for they furnished the perfect machinery to clear away fallen trees, thus allowing new trees to grow.

But when man appeared on the scene and began building houses of dead wood, the termites ate the houses with equal relish. In addition, they ate furniture, picture frames and books, and even enlarged their natural diet to include rugs and clothes.

Termite society is divided into distinct classes, and each class has its specific duties.

The king and queen live in a large, vaulted palace deep down inside the city. From the moment a queen is installed on the throne, workers begin to feed her.

Throughout the rest of her life — possibly as long as ten years — she never stops eating. In a short time she grows a thousand times as large as the king or any of her subjects — to about the size of a sausage.

But as she constantly eats, she lays a constant stream of eggs, several millions each year. Every egg is cleaned by a nurse and carried away to an incubator to hatch. In this way the queen is the actual mother of all the teeming swarms of termites in the city. When she becomes too old to lay eggs, she is killed by being starved to death, and a new queen ascends the throne.

As the huge queen lies helpless — for, of course, with her great size she cannot move — she is surrounded by a guard of soldiers, extra-large termites with heavy, sharp pincers. This guard is regularly changed every few hours, just like the guard at Buckingham Palace.

Smaller soldiers act as city policemen, keeping order among the workers and making sure that traffic moves briskly through the busy streets.

Most of the termites in the city are workers, and they are smaller than either the soldiers or police. They build the roads and bridges, gather the food, and feed the soldiers and police as well as the king and queen. Only the workers are able to feed themselves.

MOLE

STAR-NOSED MOLE

Animals That Live in the Earth

A GREAT many kinds of wild animals build their homes underground.

Many of them — like rabbits, porcupines, field mice and muskrats — spend most of their active hours on the surface and go into their burrows only to sleep, raise their families, and escape from enemies.

Others — such as woodchucks, chipmunks, prairie dogs, and burrowing snakes — roam about in the open hunting for food in warm weather, and then descend into their snug underground homes to hibernate all winter.

A few — notably moles, shrews, and gophers — live practically all their lives in the perpetual darkness of underground tunnels and nests. The outdoor world of fresh air and sunshine is foreign to them. They are afraid of it, and so they avoid it.

Moles

The common mole — that pesky little creature which ruins so many fine lawns by tunneling close to the surface and killing the grass — was designed by Nature to be the perfect digging machine. It has a small pointed head, a tapering, streamlined body, and huge front paws with which it literally swims through the earth. Its nostrils are on the sides of its nose, so that loose dirt can't clog them. It has keen hearing but no external ears, for they would get in its way. It is blind, but then it has no use for eyes in its lightless world.

The front paws of the mole are extremely large and strong and are equipped with heavy claws. The palms are twisted so that they face out, not down. The mole extends them in front of its face, like a swimmer, and its powerful shoulder muscles push the dirt aside as it moves forward through the tunnel. Its hind feet are webbed in order to kick the loose earth behind it. It can make its way through solid ground at about 12 to 15 feet an hour.

The mole's digging instinct is so much a part of its life that, even when it is asleep, it works its shovel-like paws in a slow digging motion as though dreaming that it was back on the never-ending job.

Moles build permanent nests from one to two feet deep, and then dig tunnels out in every direction in search of food. Their diet consists chiefly of earthworms and insect larvae. One naturalist investigated a mole's den in which more than a thousand earthworms were hung up on the walls, like sides of beef in a butcher shop, to provide the mole with meat on days when hunting might be bad.

The *star-nosed mole* looks like an ordinary mole that is busy eating a starfish or a small octopus. On the tip of its nose, like the petals of a daisy, is a fringe of long tentacles which constantly squirm and writhe about as it feel its way through the dark tunnels. The star-nose usually lives near lakes and rivers, and sometimes it emerges from its burrow at the water's edge and swims along the bottom searching for worms and grubs in the soft mud.

SHREW

POCKET GOPHER

Shrews

Oftentimes the hard-working mole discovers that other earth animals are sharing its underground tunnels. One of the most numerous of these uninvited guests is the nervous little shrew.

The shrew is rarely seen above ground, and when it does on occasion venture to the surface, it darts like a streak of lightning across the forest floor. But most of the time it stays down in the dark, dank world of the underground, hurrying about in its endless search for food.

The whole life pattern of the shrew is one of furious speed — not so much in its movements as in the alarming rate at which its tiny body uses up energy. Everything about the functions of the shrew's body races at a frantic pace. Its little heart hammers so rapidly that it is almost impossible to count the separate beats. Food is quickly transformed into energy, and the energy is just as quickly spent. The shrew must replenish its energy by eating a full meal at least once an hour, so it is a tireless and relentless hunter.

Shrews eat worms, grubs, seeds, roots, snails, other rodents, and almost anything else they can catch. If no other food is handy, shrews will eat each other in their desperate struggle to keep their blazing energy fueled.

For their size, shrews are the world's most vicious animals. They have been known to attack large snakes, kill them, and devour them at one sitting. In order to live, a shrew must eat three to four times its weight each day.

The shrew is the only known mammal in the world that is poisonous. It carries a venom in its saliva as deadly as that of a rattlesnake. But since the shrew has no fangs or any other means of ejecting its poison, it isn't a menace to humans. It can, however, poison a small creature by biting it and then hanging onto it until the venomous saliva seeps into the wound.

Pocket Gophers

About the only time a pocket gopher leaves its underground home is when it comes briefly to the surface to push out a load of fresh earth from its subterranean diggings. Otherwise, it is a timid little creature that much prefers the quiet darkness of its nest and tunnels. It gets its name because it has a pocket in each cheek where it carries seeds and other food to its storeroom.

Pocket gophers have a curious habit that often startles people who happen to observe it. Since their burrows are only an inch or two under the sod, they feed on the roots of flowers and other small plants. Sometimes they pull an entire plant down through the ground into their burrow.

So if you are ever sitting on a rock in the midst of a meadow in pocket-gopher country, watching the bees hum around a clump of daisies — and if suddenly one of those daisies starts to sink down into the ground inch by inch and then disappears entirely, blossom and all — you needn't think that you are seeing things. It is only a pocket gopher having a daisy salad with its dinner.

The Fantastic Fairyland of Caves

THERE IS no experience quite like that of going down into a cave for the first time. The moment you step through the cavern's entrance, you are suddenly in a fabulous fairyland world.

Fantastic icicles of stone hang from the roof in a million shapes and sizes. Tapering stone spires rise from the floor like the pipes of fairy organs. Solid rivers and waterfalls of stone flow motionless from crevices in the walls. And stone flowers, with delicate pink or yellow petals, grow in cracks between the rocks.

These are the unbelievable sights you see in caves that have been thoroughly explored, and in which electric lights have been installed so that guides can take parties of visitors through Nature's underground wonderland. But to try to explore a strange cave by yourself would be the most dangerous thing you could do, for even a few feet from its mouth a cave is totally dark.

How a Cave Is Formed

Caves are usually found in those parts of the world where the underlying rock is limestone. The chief component of limestone is calcium carbonate, the mineral *calcite,* which is readily dissolved by the small amount of carbonic acid present in practically all surface water.

A cave has its beginning when rain water seeps into the ground and flows between layers of limestone. As the water passes, it dissolves tiny parts of the stone and carries the dissolved material along with it. This ceaseless weathering of the rock by the water continues for countles thousands of years, and the pathways that the water has cut out for itself are enlarged — until at last the underlying rock is honeycombed by passageways that wind and twist down through the rock layers, and sometimes widen to form huge underground rooms.

Most large caves contain subterranean lakes and rivers, and these rivers often emerge at the surface in the form of a mighty spring — usually quite some distance from the entrance to the cave — and continue as a surface stream in the never-ending journey of water to the sea.

Stalactites and Stalagmites

When ground water seeps down through the earth, it reacts upon the limestone over which it passes and dissolves some of the *calcium carbonate* that forms the rock. As this water slowly percolates, drop by single drop, through the ceiling of a cave, each drop clings to the ceiling for a moment or so before it falls to the floor. In that short moment a slight amount of evaporation takes place, so that when the drop of water falls, it leaves behind a small solid residue of calcium carbonate.

After many centuries these tiny deposits build upon each other and eventually form a stone icicle which hangs from the ceiling. This is called a *stalactite*.

When each drop of water falls to the floor beneath the stalactite, it splashes and leaves another small deposit of calcium carbonate. These deposits gradually build upward and form a stone pillar which is called a *stalagmite*.

In the course of a long time, the hanging stalactite may join with the rising stalagmite to form a *column*. Sometimes these columns join together and divide the cave into rooms.

In places, water containing dissolved calcium carbonate flows slowly over ledges in caves, leaving deposits of the mineral behind as it evaporates. Gradually these deposits take on the form of the flowing water itself, becoming a stone waterfall.

Grains of sand on the bottom of a cave pool often have thin layers of calcite film built up around them. These lustrous round balls, sometimes as big as a man's fist, are called *cave pearls*. Now and then the water in a pool is so quiet and still that a film of calcite actually forms around a bubble. These delicate stone bubbles, so light that they float on the water, are too fragile to be picked up and will crumble at the slightest touch.

Still another kind of mineral "growth" found in caves are the beautiful and delicate clusters of *helictites*. These are caused by the same basic action as stalactites, but in some strange way the evaporation of water left these lovely flowerlike forms clinging to projecting rocks and even to the sides of stalactites.

Wind Caves

The most common types of shallow caves were formed on the sides of hills or rocky cliffs by the action of the wind and rain. This happened when a layer of soft rock, such as shale, was sandwiched between two layers of hard sandstone. Wind currents, driving rain ahead of them, swirled across the face of the hillside and scooped out the shale, often digging far back into the mountain.

Animals That Live in Caves

IT IS DIFFICULT to understand how any animal life could exist in the utter blackness of a cave. Yet many kinds of insects, fish, amphibians, mammals, and even birds live and prosper in this dark underground world.

Basically a cave has three zones of light. One is the open area just inside the entrance. Early man made his home here, and it is here that bears, mountain lions, weasels, raccoons, and other animals have their dens.

Next is a twilight zone of semidarkness which extends back into the cave for a few feet or a few hundred feet, depending upon the size of the cave opening. Here one finds the nests of owls and other night birds, and such animals as the cave rat and the tiny cave opossum.

But only a short distance from the opening, or around the first bend in the twisting passageways, the total blackness of eternal night descends upon the cave. And this black world is teeming with life.

Bats

There is probably no limestone cave of any size in the world that is not inhabited by bats. These odd animals are creatures of the night, living in the caves by day and flying out at nightfall to search for food.

Bats are the only mammals that can fly. They are the nearest living things to the pterodactyls of the age of dinosaurs. The common bat has a small furry body which looks something like that of a mouse. Its forelegs, or arms, are extremely long and thin, and the fingers of its hands are even longer than its arms. Stretching from its fingers to its feet is a thin membrane which the bat uses in the same way that a bird uses wings. Its thumb is a sharp hook by means of which it hangs to the cave wall, often upside down, when it is sleeping.

Although a bat has eyes, they are not very strong and in any case are of little use. But instead of depending on its eyes, the bat finds its way around by means of a built-in radar system. As it flies along, it sends out a continuous series of supersonic squeaks. These sound waves are reflected from solid objects to the bat's keen ears, and in this way the bat is able to avoid any obstacle that might be in its flight path.

The chief food of bats is insects, which they catch on the wing. They also scoop up water in flight.

BATS

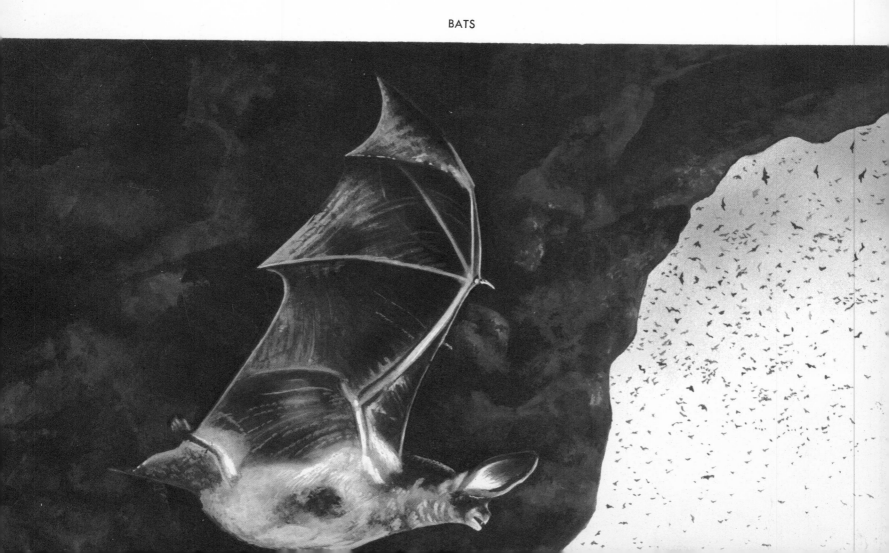

The Guacharos

While many birds nest in the twilight zone of caves, only one species lives deep within the area of total darkness. These are the amazing guacharo birds of South America.

The guacharos are huge birds, with wingspreads of about four feet. They nest by thousands high on the cave walls. Like bats, they leave the cave to hunt for food only at night, and also, like bats, they are guided through the darkness by a natural radar system.

The favorite food of guacharos is palm nuts, and flocks have been known to fly as far as sixty or seventy miles from their home cave in search of new palm groves.

Salamanders and Fish

There are a great many varieties of salamanders that live in caves all over the world. Most of them are dead white, as might be expected of amphibians that live all their lives in a world completely devoid of sunlight, but a few species have a pale pink coloring. Some have vestiges of eyes which are covered by skin. In others, the eyes have disappeared entirely.

Blind fish are found in most caves that have underground rivers and pools. They are quite small, only two or three inches long in most cases, and, like the salamanders, they are colorless. These cave fish are no doubt the descendants of surface fish that wandered into the cave rivers many hundreds of generations ago, and over the years lost their eyes because they had no use for them.

Cave Insects

The most numerous forms of life in caves are the insects. They abound in great numbers and in endless variety. There are crickets, centipedes, beetles, moths, flies, fleas and spiders. Some of the insects wander in and out of caves, but most are true cave dwellers who have adapted to life inside the earth and never emerge on the surface. Some have eyes that do not function, others have no eyes at all; but all have feelers that are long and sensitive and highly developed.

A few cave insects, in their larval stage, are luminous like glowworms. In some caves they cling to the walls and ceilings in dense masses and light up the blackness like bright stars in a moonless sky.

In certain caves in the American South there is a large fly, known as a *fungus gnat,* which is also luminous in its larval stage. But the most unusual thing about this fly is its curious unflylike habit of spinning a web in which it catches other flies — and even spiders!

GUACHARO

SALAMANDER

BLIND FISH

CAVE CRICKET

ROCK OF AGES

PEOPLE

A vaulted room in the Carlsbad Caverns

The Carlsbad Caverns

WHEN CATTLEMEN from Texas drove their herds onto the ranges of southern New Mexico in the 1880's, they were amazed to see great clouds of bats emerge each evening from a large hole in the ground a few miles north of the Guadalupe Mountains. Investigating, they discovered that the hole was the opening of what seemed to be an enormous cave, with primitive Indian pictographs painted on the entrance walls.

For several years, no one ventured more than a few feet inside the cave. Then, one day in 1901, a young cowboy let his curiosity get the better of him. With a kerosene lantern for light, he went down the steeply sloping corridors — and discovered one of the largest and most awe-inspiring limestone caves on earth.

Today the caverns are lighted throughout, and guides take more than half a million visitors each year down into the earth's depths to view the wonders of this incredible realm of fantasy.

From the entrance, the main passageway of the cave slopes sharply downward to a depth of more than 800 feet. On the way you pass clusters of millions of stalactites hanging down from the ceiling like filmy curtains of stone lace—jungles of huge stalagmites rising up from the floor like mushrooms — frozen waterfalls of stone — and weird statues sculptured by Nature in the form of totem poles, elephants, birds and pagan idols.

At the bottom, the passageways spread out into what is the largest underground room in the world. It is nearly half a mile long, at one place almost a quarter of a mile wide, and the ceiling is 285 feet high at its highest point.

Almost every square foot of the ceiling and walls is decorated with a drapery of stalactites, and the trails that wind through the Big Room pass through a forest of giant stone tree trunks as big around as houses. Clusters of helictites cling to cracks in the walls with the profusion of flowers in a summer garden.

The Caves of Ice

THERE is no end to the wonder of caves. And some of the most wonderful of all are the fantastic ice caves of the European mountains.

Ages ago, when the world's climate was much warmer than it is now, underground rivers tunneled their way into the solid mountain rock. Then the long Ice Age descended on the Northern Hemisphere, and these rivers froze in their subterranean beds. Today they still exist as caves of ice.

In places, far under the mountain tops, these ice rivers flow into ice lakes that are as smooth and flat as skating rinks. Sometimes they drop suddenly to create a solid waterfall of ice nearly half as high as Niagara.

In the open corridors of the caves, columns of ice rise from the floor like crystal stalagmites. These were created by the slow dripping and quick refreezing of melted ice falling from above. Now and then the columns fuse together to form delicately sculptured ice curtains.

Often stalactites of ice hang suspended from the ceiling of the cave, so crystal clear that they can serve as gigantic magnifying glasses. Occasionally bubbles of air were imprisoned in the stalactite when it froze, giving the huge formation the iridescent quality of a gleaming jewel.

Like glaciers, the frozen rivers of the ice caves are slowly flowing — at the rate of a few inches a year.

The Blue Grotto of Capri

SOME CAVES along the shoreline are formed by the grinding action of ocean waves on the soft rock strata of coastal cliffs. The most widely known of these sea caves is the fantastically beautiful Blue Grotto on the Isle of Capri in Italy's Bay of Naples.

The base rock from which the grotto was cut is a limestone formation, but it was not worn away by the action of surface water as are true limestone caves like the Carlsbad Caverns. Instead, the endless pounding of the surf on the rocks carved out the cave by erosion.

All sea caves are generally shallow, but the Blue Grotto is one of the world's largest. It is 175 feet long, 98 feet wide, and 50 feet high. However, the roof at the entrance is only three feet above the water line and very narrow, so that the cave may be entered only in a small boat.

The bright sunshine of southern Italy fills the grotto with a brilliant blue light that reflects off the myriad stalactites hanging from the ceiling and walls in a dazzling display of color.

An ice cave in Spain

The Blue Grotto of Capri

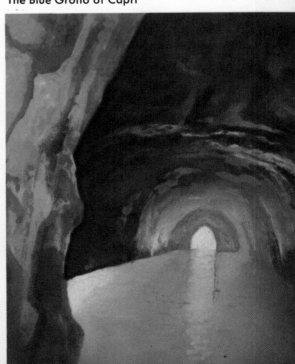

Cave Exploration

MOST of us are content to limit our exploration of caves to those like the Carlsbad Caverns, or Mammoth Cave in Kentucky, which are well lighted throughout, have stairways and paved trails, and are open to the public for sightseeing tours conducted by experienced guides.

But under the right circumstances—with proper planning and equipment and the guidance of experts—cave exploring can be an exciting, though sometimes a risky, hobby.

Of course, there have always been people with a deep-seated curiosity about caves, and today cave exploring has become a popular sport.

Amateur cave explorers call themselves spelunkers—after the Latin word for "cave," *spelunca*. Like most other sports enthusiasts, they join together in clubs. This enables them to share the cost of equipment and travel and to go on exploring expeditions in groups.

When they are exploring a strange, or "wild," cave, spelunkers usually rope themselves together. For the first safety rule of all spelunker clubs is: *Never go into a wild cave alone.* The second rule is: *Never go cave exploring without proper equipment.* This means adequate lights, ropes, hard hats, warm clothing, and heavy nonskid shoes.

Many important cave discoveries have been made by amateur spelunker groups. One of the most dramatic of these finds took place only a few years ago near the town of Grenoble in France.

There was a deep opening on a hillside in a farmer's pasture which natives had avoided for years, calling it "the bottomless pit." A French spelunking club decided to investigate.

Very cautiously, roped together for safety, they descended into the hole, which opened out into a series of underground rooms a short way beneath the surface. But always there was a steep descent or a hole that went deeper.

Slowly, carefully, they made their way farther into the depths — through narrow chimneys in the rock, past swift-flowing underground rivers, around roaring waterfalls, down the sides of perpendicular cliffs. At times they squeezed their bodies through cracks in the rock that were only a foot or two wide, and then when they got through, discovered themselves in vast, high-ceilinged rooms.

At last the party reached a level that was 2,963 feet below the surface—more than half a mile underground—the deepest point to which man had ever penetrated into a cave. From here a deeper hole dropped even farther into the black depths. But there seemed to be no safe passageway into it—so the spelunkers were content to let their world record stand.

Underwater Caves

SINCE limestone caves are created by the action of underground water, it is not surprising that many of them are permanently flooded. This means that spelunkers who wish to explore them must equip themselves with aqualungs, instead of ropes and ladders. Such a submarine cavern is Wakulla Cave in northwestern Florida.

Wakulla Spring, source of the Wakulla River, is a small lake fed entirely by underground water. For a long time, geologists reasoned that the water supply must come from a vast subterranean reservoir. But nothing definite was known about it until recently, when a group of college students—all experienced skin-divers—resolved to find out what lay beneath the spring's surface.

When they were finished, they had discovered the most sensational water cave in the world—and made a number of puzzling fossil finds as well.

Underneath the placid surface of the spring, the cave slanted sharply downward to a depth of nearly 200 feet, and there it began to level off. Its width varied from about 70 to 150 feet, and its height from floor to ceiling was in places only 5 feet and in others more than 100 feet. The floor was of sand, with patches of clay and limestone rubble.

The divers explored the cavern to a distance of 1,100 feet from the entrance. Here the bottom began to drop sharply into what appeared to be a much wider and deeper section of the cave. But the explorers could not remain under water long enough to go beyond this point. It is probable that Wakulla Cave may extend for miles.

As important to scientists as the discovery of the cave itself were strange fossil remains that the divers found.

Two hundred feet inside the entrance, and about the same distance below the surface, they came upon bones of mammoths, mastodons, giant sloths, and prehistoric deer. Included was a mastodon tusk, in nearly perfect condition, which weighed several hundred pounds. In the same place, more than five hundred bone spearheads—of the kind used by Florida's prehistoric cave men—were scattered over the sandy floor.

Scientists are still puzzling over the problem of how these relics reached the depth and position inside the cave at which they were found. The way in which the bones and artifacts occur suggests that the cave was dry when they got into the cave.

The most likely answer lies in the changing level of the ocean during the ice age. The glaciers spreading across the more polar lands were nourished by water extracted by evaporation from the sea. Sea level dropped 300 feet or more as a result during the great advances. This drop of the sea would allow the water table on land to drop also and thus expose the Wakulla Cave to air and allow animals and man to enter.

Skin divers exploring Wakulla Cave in Florida

Cave Paintings From the Ice Age

ONE FALL afternoon, not quite a hundred years ago, a man named Don Marcellino de Sautuola and his little daughter, Maria, set out to explore a cave that had recently been discovered on a farm called Altamira in northern Spain. Don Marcellino was an amateur archeologist, and he knew that such caves often contained stone weapons and other implements of the ancient people who had lived in them thousands of years before.

Arriving at the cave, Don Marcellino gave Maria a candle, warned her not to stray too far into the dark cavern, and then began digging through the rubble.

The little girl poked around through all the nooks and crannies of the main cave and then, holding her candle before her, she wandered down a narrow, twisting corridor into the absolute blackness of the cave's interior.

In a few minutes Don Marcellino heard her terrified scream from deep within the cave:

"Bulls! Daddy! Bulls! Come quick!"

Don Marcellino dropped his digging tools and rushed down the passageway. He rounded one turn after another and came at last to a large room where his daughter stood pointing a shaking hand at the ceiling. There he saw a sight such as no modern man had ever seen before.

Painted on the low ceiling of the cave—in brilliant shades of red, brown, violet, yellow, black, and white—was the magnificent picture reproduced on the opposite page and many others like it. The animals were bison — very much like the buffalo of the American plains — and they were painted with an artistic perfection that would do justice to any modern artist.

Don Marcellino could hardly believe his eyes. There was a whole herd of the beasts, eighteen in all. Some were standing, some were running and jumping, others were lying quietly as though asleep. He touched one of the animals. The paint was as fresh-looking and bright as if the artist had completed the work only yesterday!

Even more amazing was the fact that there was not a single smudge of soot on the entire ceiling!

Don Marcellino called in professors from the University of Madrid and other leading art centers to examine the strange and weirdly beautiful cave paintings, and for many years a furious controversy raged about the bison of Altamira. Most critics instantly dismissed them as fakes. But at last their authenticity was established— although a great many questions about the paintings have gone unanswered to this day.

There have been no bison in Spain since the Ice Age —but obviously the artist had studied the animals closely. Therefore the paintings must have been done by a highly skilled cave man no more recently than twenty or twenty-five thousand years ago.

The Altamira cave had been hermetically sealed by a landslide at the end of the Ice Age, and it had not reopened until a few months before Don Marcellino and Maria visited it. This would explain the remarkable freshness of the painting.

But—

Why did the artist select the deep, absolutely dark interior of a cave as a place to do his work?

How did he provide light to see by—since there was no smudge of soot or smoke on the walls?

What strange race of ancient man had developed his artistic techniques to the level of modern-day painters?

Where did they get their paints, and how did they apply them?

No one has yet come up with all the answers. All we know is that the paintings were done by some unknown genius at least twenty thousand years ago.

A few years later, a similar group of prehistoric paintings were found in a cave near the village of La Mouthe in France. Again the artist had drawn bison—as well as antelopes and reindeer. And again, these were animals that had not lived in Europe since the Ice Age!

As in the case of Altamira, the cave at La Mouthe had been sealed off by a landslide ages ago, so the paintings were fresh and clear.

Now the search for Ice Age cave paintings was on in earnest. And scientists began to find them all over the world.

In Mtoko Cave, in Southern Rhodesia, they came upon an amazing wild life scene containing elephants, antelopes, buffaloes, crocodiles, trees, plants, and human hunters — as well as mystical religious symbols. They found others in South Africa, Norway, Italy, Libya, Australia, and the southwestern United States.

What strange urge prompted primitive man to create rock paintings deep inside the pitch-black interior of caves? Why did this urge come upon him in so many different parts of the world at about the same time in archeological history—some twenty thousand years ago?

It is quite probable that no one will ever completely solve the riddle.

"Bulls! Daddy! Come quick!"

The Primitive Cave Men

IT WAS only natural that ancient man should live in caves. He had neither the tools nor the skills to build houses or even crude huts, so hillside caves provided shelters from cold, snow, rain, and wild beasts.

As far as we can determine, man has been living on the earth for more than half a million years and evidence in caves has traced his history to about 100,000 B.C.

At that time man didn't look very much as he does today. He was short—not much more than five feet tall. He was heavy and squat, with stubby legs and long, thick arms. He had a low sloping forehead, little beady eyes, a massive apelike jaw, and a receding chin. Most of his body was probably covered with a thick mat of hair.

His only tools were crude hatchets and knives made of flint. He was just learning to use fire to warm the inside of his cave, although he probably used it for nothing else. His only clothing was the skin of animals he killed for food. He knew nothing of planting crops or keeping domestic animals.

Human beings of this long-ago period were called Neanderthal Man, because the first traces of their remains were discovered in the Neanderthal Valley in Germany.

A few years ago a team of American archeologists, digging in a cave on a rocky hillside in the Zagros Mountains of Iraq, unearthed a continuous history of man's progress from the Neanderthal period to the present day.

Shanidar Cave, as they called it, goes about 150 feet into the side of the hill and is roughly the same distance wide. It has a high ceiling and a level packed-down floor of earth and sand. Today it is inhabited by a tribe of Kurdish goatherds, who have built huts inside its protecting walls, as well as pens for their goats and chickens.

But the amazing thing about Shanidar Cave is the fact that it has been almost continuously inhabited by man for about 100,000 years! And the whole story of man's progress during that time can be read in the layers of debris packed under the cave floor.

Luckily for scientists, the tenants of the cave, from the earliest times, were very untidy housekeepers. Instead of sweeping out their trash and refuse, they simply buried it under succeeding layers of dust and dirt. Thus, by digging down into the floor of the cave, the archeologists were able to lay bare a cross section of human history — in much the same way that fossils in layers of rock can give us a picture history of the earth itself.

The scientists found four main layers of packed-down dirt and debris under the cave floor — each one representing a definite period in the history of man's progress.

The top layer dates from the present time to about 7,000 years ago. Here the archeologists found pieces of pottery, stones for grinding grain, the bones of domestic animals — all evidence that by this time man was learning to grow his own crops and tend his own herds.

Below this was a layer that radioactive measurements indicated to be some 12,000 years old. There was no indication here that the people of this period knew anything about farming or pottery making. There were, however, a number of bone spearheads and even bone needles which were probably used to sew fur into clothes.

The third layer went further back in time to about 40,000 B.C., according to radioactivity measurements of the charcoal from ancient fire pits. Yet in all of the nearly 30,000 years that intervened between this layer and the one above it, there was little evidence that man had made much progress in his way of living.

Finally, the fourth and last layer of the accumulated debris on the floor of Shanidar Cave takes the history of mankind back about 100,000 years.

Over the long eons, earthquakes had shaken rock fragments loose from the cave's ceiling and killed some of the inhabitants. Like the other debris in the cave, these unhappy people were also buried under the endless piling up of layers of dirt and soil.

The first skeleton discovered was that of a man who died 45,000 years ago. A second, found farther down, had been killed 15,000 years earlier than that. And then, almost at the bottom of the uttermost layer of dirt, diggers unearthed the skeleton of a little child who was crushed by a rock fall more than 70,000 years ago.

It is from such bits and pieces of evidence—excavated from the floors of caves in all parts of the world—that we are able to piece together a picture of the life of Neanderthal Man at the dawn of human history.

If we close our eyes, we can see him now—huddled over a flickering fire in the mouth of his cave—wrapped in raw fur against the Ice Age cold—possibly chopping out a crude flint hatchet with which to kill a bison or a reindeer—and never dreaming that on some far-distant day his remote descendants might be wondering what his everyday life was like.

Cave man making primitive stone tools

The cliff cities of Mesa Verde, Colorado

The Cliff Dwellers

PERHAPS the most interesting and unusual of all the ancient peoples who lived in caves were the cliff dwellers of the American Southwest. They built villages of stone, perched like eagles' nests under overhanging ledges of rock hundreds of feet high on sheer canyon walls. And here they developed a way of life that was surprisingly modern.

These cliff villages—the largest of which are in Mesa Verde National Park in Colorado—were first built nearly two thousand years ago. The high cliffside caves offered perfect protection not only from the elements but from wild animals and human enemies as well.

Until about seven hundred years ago, the dry desert country of southwestern Colorado was a little greener than it is now, with enough annual rainfall for agriculture. So the Indians cultivated thriving farms on the tops of the mesas above their cliffs. Here they also pastured the flocks of turkeys that they had domesticated, and hunted deer, bear, and mountain sheep.

Under the projecting shelves of the cliffs, the Indians constructed stone buildings, two, three, or sometimes four stories high. Most of them were "apartment houses," some with as many as two hundred rooms, with one family living in each room. The rooms were small, but they had neatly plastered walls, most of which were decorated with paintings.

In addition to living quarters, the cliff villages contained granaries for storing the harvest of corn, beans and squash, and ceremonial rooms for religious rites.

The individual houses were built on shelves of the cliff, usually around a broad central patio. They were joined to each other by balconies and terraces, with high protective walls to keep the children from tumbling over into the bottom of the canyon 700 or 800 feet below. Steps chopped out of the sheer cliff walls connected the various levels of the town and also led up to the farms on the mesa above.

Many of the houses had springs of fresh water which dripped down through the layers of rock. The cooking was done in the open on the terraces. The women ground dried corn into meal with stone rolling pins, and baked cornbread on thin rock slabs laid over the fire.

The cliff dwellers developed a highly organized system of industry. Most of them were specialists in some particular craft, just as modern workers are today. Some made bowls, pots, urns, and jars from the clay of the canyon bottoms. Others wove cloth from the cotton grown on the farms. Still others made bows and arrows for hunting and chopped out knives, hatchets, and other cutting tools from flint and quartz.

Metal was unknown to the cliff dwellers, and thus all their stone-cutting was done with tools made of harder stone. Yet in spite of this handicap they were skilled masons, and the walls, which they built of sandstone slabs held together by adobe mortar, show hardly a crack.

They wove baskets and mats of reeds and grass, and made sturdy ropes from the fibers of yucca plants. The more skillful artisans carved beads and other jewelry from shells and rock crystals. Like most other Indian tribes, the cliff dwellers used strings of beads as money.

Artists decorated the smooth sandstone walls of the cliffs with curious paintings and carvings of men, animals, birds, and religious symbols. Some of their most puzzling pictures are those of human handprints—as though the artist had wet his hand with water, pressed it to the stone, and then carved out the outline.

The cliff dwellers had a curious way of burying their dead. They stuffed them into cracks and crannies far back in the caves behind the houses, and covered them up with dust, dirt, ashes, and trash. These materials gradually drew out all the moisture from the flesh, and in the hot, dry Colorado climate the bodies became mummified. Many of these mummies are perfectly preserved today, shrunken and shriveled, but remarkably lifelike.

By a curious freak of nature, we can tell almost exactly to the year when the civilization of the cliff dwellers, which had flourished for so many centuries, came to an abrupt end. The tragic story can be pieced together by examining the growth rings of trees that grew during that period. In the year 1276, more than two centuries before Columbus landed on the shores of the New World, a great drought struck this part of the Southwest. No rain fell. The crops withered and died. The grass dried up and the wild game left the area. The springs of water went dry. The rivers that had carved out the canyons ceased to flow.

This period of famine lasted for twenty-four years. During this time the Indians reluctantly turned their backs on their fine cliffside cities and sought other lands to the south and southwest.

Modern Cave Dwellers

The Cone City of Cappadocia

IN THE remote regions of Cappadocia, deep in the heart of Turkey's Anatolian highlands, lies the curious city of the cones.

Scores of thousands of years ago a now-extinct volcano, Erciyas Dagi, spewed out vast quantities of ash and molten lava which covered the countryside for miles around with a fiery blanket hundreds of feet thick. As this mass of soft, rocklike material cooled and hardened, it began to crack. Then pelting rains and melting snows and driving winds widened the cracks and carved the high places between them into thousands of jagged pinnacles and cones which jutted up from the valley floor.

In the early days of Christianity, some time between the fifth and twelfth centuries, a group of monks came to the valley. It contained no wood or other building material, and since the rock pillars were soft enough to be readily carved, the monks hollowed out the cones to make their monasteries and chapels.

The curious cone houses of Cappadocia

A cave village in Andalusia

Some of these temples were elaborately sculptured, with huge columns at the entrances and high domes inside which were covered with sacred paintings. The monks cut spiral stairways and slanted ramps and tunnels that led to rooms on upper levels, and so created buildings that are as much as ten stories high.

No one knows exactly who these monks were, or where they came from, or why. We know only that they must have lived in their carved-out colony for several hundred years. Then, just as mysteriously as they had appeared, they abandoned the valley. And there is no record of why they did so or where they went.

In any case, Turkish farmers moved into the valley an uncertain number of years later, established farms on the level ground between the cones, and took over the strange rock dwellings as their homes.

The lava ash of the valley makes it very fertile. Here these primitive farmers grow thriving crops of vegetables, grain, and fruit. Herds of sheep and goats graze on the green slopes, and the smaller cones are used as stables in the winter months.

On the inside, the cone houses look very much like the homes of any other Turkish farmers, although the rooms are considerably larger than those in a conventional dwelling. They have another great advantage in that, being hewn from solid rock, they are cool in the hot Turkish summers and warm in the frigid Turkish winters.

The fireplaces are primitive, and so smoke quickly blackens the ceilings and walls. Once each year the women clean house by chipping away the sooty layer of rock. This not only cleans the room, but enlarges it slightly. Then they cover the surface of the ceilings and walls with a fresh coat of whitewash.

The Cave Dwellers of Andalusia

ANDALUSIA, a province of southern Spain that borders the Mediterranean Sea, is a land of high coastal mountains which slope down to the interior plain in a series of rolling foothills. These hills are mostly of limestone formation, and are honeycombed with thousands of caves.

About five hundred years ago, tribes of nomadic gypsies from the Near East wandered into this part of Spain and roamed from town to town earning their living as peddlers, tinkers, fortunetellers, and dancers. But when they came to the old cities of Granada and Gaudix, they saw that the hillside caves could serve as ready-built houses. And so many of them settled there.

They smoothed out the cave walls, leveled the stone floors, sealed up the cave openings to allow space for only a single door and sometimes a small window—and in time created a number of cave villages.

Like the cones of Cappadocia, the cave houses of Andalusia have natural air-conditioning. They are cool and pleasant in summer and provide perfect protection against the bitter winds of winter.

Today these cave houses dot the Andalusian hillsides. They are of all kinds and sizes. Some have only a single room with a blanket for a door, while others are elaborate affairs with twenty rooms or more on two or three levels.

The Andalusian caves have been made into big high-ceilinged churches, schools, shops, stores, and cafés as well as homes. The spires of the churches protrude upward through the surface, as do the chimneys of the houses.

Tunnels

MAN'S mightiest efforts at burrowing tunnels under the earth will never equal the total length of those dug every year by such of Nature's engineers as the mole, the earthworm, and the ant. But, even so, man has been digging tunnels since the dawn of time.

Prehistoric cave men dug tunnels to enlarge their primitive homes and to reach deposits of flint for making tools and weapons. Traces of these tunnels have been found in the chalk districts of England. However, the first major tunnel was built by the Assyrians about 2000 B.C. to divert the water of the Euphrates River. And the Bible tells how King Hezekiah constructed a tunnel to bring water to Jerusalem in the seventh century B.C.

The Romans were the most skillful of the ancient tunnel builders. In addition to numerous aqueducts which supplied their cities with water, they built a great many tunnels to carry vehicular traffic. One of the most impressive of these is the Posilipo Tunnel near Naples, which was built in 36 B.C. and is still in use today. It is more than half a mile long and is 75 feet wide at the entrances.

In Hyderabad, India, generations of Buddhist priests worked for nearly a thousand years at the monumental task of tunneling cave temples out of the living bedrock. The high-vaulted temples, huge idols, life-size elephants, and towering obelisks were all carved in one piece.

During the Middle Ages, the science of engineering declined, and the only tunnels dug were for military purposes. When an army attacked a city, its soldiers tunneled under the walls and shored up the sides of the tunnel with wooden beams. When the tunnel was completed, the beams were set on fire, and the tunnel collapsed, causing the city walls above it to fall in.

Perhaps the most famous of all military tunnels was the one dug under the Confederate defenses at Petersburg, Virginia, during the Civil War. When it was completed, the tunnel was 510 feet long. It was then charged with 8,000 pounds of gunpowder. The mine exploded as planned, blowing a tremendous crater in the center of the Confederate line. But Federal generals got their orders confused and failed to take advantage of the break before the Southern forces re-formed their lines.

The great era of tunnel building came with the development of railroads in the nineteenth century. A horse and carriage could climb over a mountain but a railway train couldn't. As might be expected, railroad tunneling had its beginnings in the Alps.

In 1857 work was started on the Mont Cenis Tunnel, the first of these Alpine undertakings. In the beginning the workmen dug at the rock wall of the mountain by hand, and the tunnel progressed at the rate of only a few inches a day. As the years dragged by, new tunneling techniques were developed, such as compressed-air drills and the use of blasting powder. The tunnel was at last completed in 1871. It is eight miles long, the fourth longest railway tunnel in the world today.

The world's longest railway tunnel is the Simplon Tunnel, which winds through the Alps for more than twelve miles between Switzerland and Italy. In places it is 7,000 feet under the mountain peak. The longest in the United States is the New Cascade Tunnel in Washington, nearly eight miles in length.

The longest tunnel of any kind ever dug is the Delaware Aqueduct which carries water from the mountains to New York City. It is 85 miles from end to end.

Underwater Tunnels

TUNNELING through the solid rock of a mountain is a difficult and dangerous job, but it is relatively easy compared to digging under the soft mud of a river. Underwater tunneling is usually made possible only with the use of a compressed-air shield. This is a steel cylinder, about the same size as the tunnel that is to be built, into which compressed air is forced to prevent cave-ins and to keep water from seeping in and flooding the diggings. As workmen excavate ahead of the shield, it is pushed forward to provide a lining for the tunnel.

The first underwater tunnel in America, between New York City and New Jersey, was completed in 1904. Today more than a dozen underwater tunnels connect New York City with its suburbs.

As this is written, preliminary work has already begun on what is probably the greatest engineering project ever undertaken—a tunnel under the English Channel which will go from England to France. When completed, it will have a double-track rail line 36 miles long. Ventilation problems will make an automobile tunnel impossible, but autos will be carried on railway flatcars while the passengers ride inside the train itself.

Traffic entrance to tunnel under English Channel, which will connect London and Paris

CLIFFS OF DOVER

TUNNEL VENTILATION TOWERS

FOLKESTONE

HELIPORT

PASSENGER PLATFORM

PASSENGER TERMINAL

AUTOMOBILE LOADING BUILDING

AUTOMOBILE TERMINAL BUILDING

EXPRESS TRAIN PARIS TO LONDON

ADMINISTRATION BUILDING

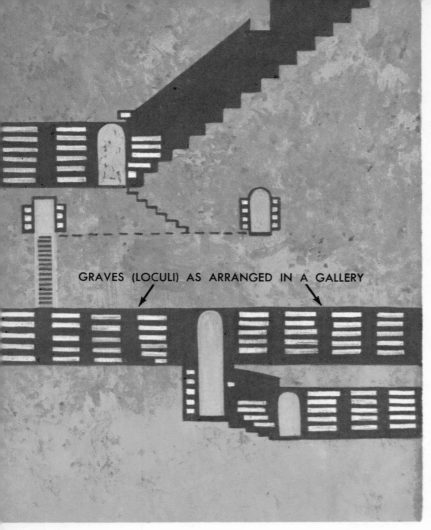

GRAVES (LOCULI) AS ARRANGED IN A GALLERY

A section of the Roman catacombs,
showing galleries at different levels

Wall painting from individual tomb

The Catacombs of Rome

NEXT to the Gospels themselves, our best understanding of the beliefs, customs, and way of life of the early Christians comes from a study of the inscriptions and the works of art in the ancient catacombs— that great maze of tunnels and manmade caves that lies under a large part of the modern city of Rome.

For the first three hundred years after the crucifixion of Christ, Christianity was outlawed in the Roman Empire. People who were known to be believers in the new religion were imprisoned, sold into slavery, or put to death. The Emperor Nero blamed the Christians for the burning of Rome in A.D. 64 and thus began a wave of merciless persecution that lasted for nearly three centuries.

As a result, all Christian religious ceremonies had to be conducted in secret. This applied even to the sacred rite of burying the dead. Like so many minority groups both before and since, the Christians literally went underground.

During this period, a great many wealthy Romans had

secretly embraced the Christian faith. It w
who provided the money for the first of
or underground burial places, in and arou

The rock strata underlying Rome ar
both sedimentary and volcanic rock. The
rocks were valued by the Romans for
and were therefore extensively quarr
deposits were of no use to the Ro
and it was in these that the Chr
burial caves.

This rock was volcanic tufa. It was
dug out with picks and shovels; yet onc it wa
and exposed to the air, it hardened to about t'
tency of a porous cement. The workmen who
catacombs toiled under very difficult con
their work in secret, by the dim light
lamps, and they had to carry the excavate
in baskets and dispose of it where the
find it.

The entrances to the catacombs w

which could be hidden by a pile of stones—
urial tunnels extended for long distances under-
nd were often as many as six levels in depth.

year 313, the Emperor Constantine formally
d the Christian religion, so that the Christians
rship openly. From this time on, the catacombs
as burial vaults, and became shrines and places
p to which pilgrims came to venerate the relics
rly martyrs.

he need for secrecy over, the entrances to the
s were enlarged. Wide stairways went down
nderground crypts, and the openings were often
ed by a chapel or a church. The caves themselves
anded to allow for large galleries and halls
which processions of priests and worshipers
on holy days and sang mass by candlelight in
y corridors.

heir beginnings, the walls of the catacombs and
of the tombs had been decorated with paintings
arprisingly brilliant colors. Most of them depict
in the life of Jesus—the adoration of the Magi,
m of Jesus, the miracle of the loaves and fishes,
ng of the sick, and many more. Other pictures
stories from the Old Testament—Daniel in the
, Moses leading the Jews out of Egypt, and
he ark.

Other catacomb paintings symbolize Jesus as a lamb, as a good shepherd, and, strangely enough, as a fish. The fish symbol was the recognition sign of the early Christians, and it was arrived at in a curious manner. If you write the Greek words meaning "Jesus Christ of God the Son, our Saviour," the initials of each word form the Greek word *ichthys,* meaning "fish."

The symbol of the cross does not appear in any of the art of the catacombs. In Roman times, crucifixion was a form of punishment reserved for only the lowest criminals. Thus, to the early Christians, the cross was a sign of humiliation. It was not until centuries later that the cross became the most sacred of all Christian symbols.

In addition to religious art, a great many other artifacts have been found in the catacombs. Chief among these are the "gold glasses"—crystal goblets decorated with gold leaf, which were used at wedding feasts and funeral banquets. They were usually pressed into the fresh plaster of the catacomb walls to identify their owner's burial place. Other objects from the ancient days are combs and buttons of carved ivory and bone, as well as children's toys.

In about the ninth century the catacombs of Rome were abandoned as places of worship and forgotten. They were not rediscovered and fully explored as cradles of religious history until about a hundred years ago.

nobleman's tomb

New York's Fabulous "Underworld"

ANTS and termites aren't the only creatures that live and work in underground communities. One of man's largest communities is also entirely beneath the earth's surface. It has thousands of stores, shops, restaurants, amusement centers, banks, post offices—and even its own police force. And it is serviced by hundreds of miles of underground railway tracks.

This is the subsurface half of New York, a fantastic underground city that has grown up around the subway system.

The New York subways rank as one of the greatest engineering feats of all time. The tunnels honeycomb the bedrock of Manhattan Island, often on three or four levels. They wind in and out and up and down, passing over and under each other as they crisscross the island. There are few places in New York that can't be reached by subway in a very short time.

Every year the subways carry 1,355,000,000 passengers, more than three times as many as all the United States railroads put together. Yet despite the passenger traffic and the high speed at which the trains travel, an enviable record of safety in transportation has been built up for more than thirty years.

The world's first subway was built in London during the 1860's, but it was a very uncomfortable and unpopular means of transportation. Trains had to be pulled through the tunnels by steam engines, and the smoke made traveling underground almost unbearable. This was the chief reason why a subway system for New York was turned down when it was first suggested at about the same time, though the city even then was rapidly running out of space for its people to move about in.

Instead, elevated railways were constructed to ease the city's growing traffic problem. The "Els" were smoky and dirty, but at least they were more comfortable than riding through a tunnel behind an engine that puffed out great stifling clouds of black coal smoke.

Yet the men who dreamed of subways for New York didn't give up their dreams easily. One inventor, Alfred E. Beach — without bothering to get permission from the city authorities — secretly built a tunnel 312 feet long, under a block in downtown New York. He fitted it up with a train which he blew back and forth from one end of the short line to the other with gusts of compressed air. In 1869 he opened it to the public, but a ride of only a hundred yards didn't do much to ease New York's traffic jam, and so America's pioneer subway was soon forgotten.

By the end of the nineteenth century, however, the electric locomotive had been developed. Now that the ideal means for underground travel was at last available, construction began on New York's first subway line in the year 1900.

It extended a little more than twenty miles, from City Hall in lower Manhattan to the Bronx. But long before it was completed in 1904, lines connecting other parts of the city were already under construction.

Today the subway system is literally the main artery of New York. Without it, the city's seven million people would be unable to get from their homes to the places where they work.

During the peak rush hours, in the mornings and evenings, 9,000 trains are in continuous operation. There are 486 stations which are open day and night.

It is in the larger stations — Times Square, Grand Central, Pennsylvania Station, Rockefeller Center — that the subway system takes on the aspect of an underground city. In the miles of streets and underground shopping centers of these big stations can be found practically every product and service offered on the surface.

Alfred E. Beach's subway.
It didn't go far enough!

Many of the world's largest cities have subways — London, Paris, Moscow, Berlin. But it is only in New York that the subways have extended themselves into a truly subterranean world. From a subway you can go into America's largest theater, Radio City Music Hall. You can enter dozens of New York's finest hotels, the world's largest department stores and the finest specialty shops by an underground entrance. In fact, it would be possible for a person to live in the underground city of the subway system all of his life without venturing even once into New York's sunlight!

Here is a cross section of a typical New York subway station. It is located at 42nd Street between Park and Lexington avenues.

At top center is the street-level entrance to the Hotel Commodore. Below it is the entrance to the subway. At the extreme left (top) is the elevated highway for automobiles that carries Park Avenue around and through the Grand Central Building.

The first underground level contains stores, shops, and restaurants, as well as the turnstiles at the entrance to the subway platforms. The long moving stairway on the right of the first level leads down to a second level where trains leave for other destinations. Underneath it, a tunnel leads to another part of the station.

At the extreme lower right, stairs lead down to still a third level — and still another set of tracks that help make up New York's fabulous underworld.

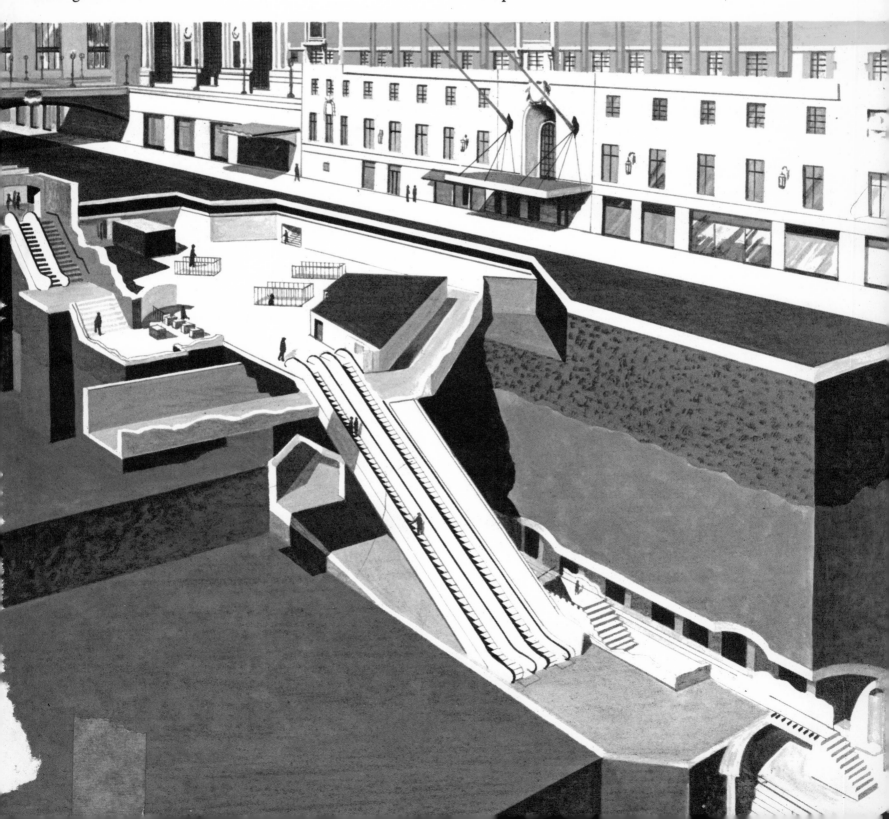

Index